NEGOTIATION SKILLS
FOR VIRGINS

Bob Etherington

Marshall Cavendish
Business

First published in 2008
This edition published in 2018 by Marshall Cavendish Business
An imprint of Marshall Cavendish International

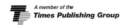

A member of the
Times Publishing Group

Other Marshall Cavendish Offices:
Marshall Cavendish Corporation. 99 White Plains Road, Tarrytown NY 10591-
9001, USA • Marshall Cavendish International (Thailand) Co Ltd. 253 Asoke,
12th Flr, Sukhumvit 21 Road, Klongtoey Nua, Wattana, Bangkok 10110,
Thailand • Marshall Cavendish (Malaysia) Sdn Bhd, Times Subang, Lot 46,
Subang Hi-Tech Industrial Park, Batu Tiga, 40000 Shah Alam, Selangor Darul
Ehsan, Malaysia

National Library Board Singapore Cataloguing-in-Publication Data

Name(s): Etherington, Bob.
Title: Negotiating skills for virgins / Bob Etherington.
Description: Singapore : Marshall Cavendish Business, 2018. |
First published: 2008.
Identifier(s): OCN 1014491356 | ISBN 978-981-4794-69-5 (paperback)
Subject(s): LCSH: Negotiation in business. | Negotiation.
Classification: DDC 658.4052--dc23

Cover design by Lorraine Aw

Printed in Singapore by Fabulous Printers Pte Ltd

Contents

Warning:
Before You Buy This Book ...

The material you have in your hands is very valuable.

There are many people who do (or would like to do) business with you, who would rather you didn't have it. It is an unusually practical book about the real secrets of negotiating some "really" great deals for yourself.

It has been written for people like you (often, in my experience, from the Northern Hemisphere) who feel that they are probably terrible at negotiating and would like to do it better! ... well ... OK, "brilliantly well".

But first ...

I said in the first paragraph the real secrets of negotiating. But maybe you believe that you have seen it or read it all before. So first a self-test to see whether you are ready for the material in this book; please answer this question:

Which do you think is the longest line in the diagram below? Line A or line B?

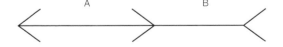

So which is it then ... "A" or "B"? I know you've seen it, or similar diagrams, before in countless children's comics and books of optical illusion but give me your answer anyway. "They're both the same length," you say. Very good. You know that's right because you've seen it before, like I said.

But now I'd like you, if you would, to actually measure the two lines. Go on, please do it now ... if you're standing in a bookshop use the edge of a bus/train/plane ticket.

Oh dear! I know! You've just discovered line A is 30% longer than line B!

But all we "adults" do it all the time ... me too. Whatever it is, we think we've seen it (read it or heard it) all before and we "assume" we know. And you may think this book is also one that is going to be full of stuff you already know. However I'd like to open your mind to the unexpected.

This is a book born out of several years of practical and successful negotiating around the world. The approach has been used, by me, to negotiate the sale and purchase of personal artefacts (cars, houses, TVs) and, in the work-world, to seal deals on mutually favourable terms (redundancy packages, salary increases, international contracts worth several million).

So I'd like you to suspend your adult scepticism and reinforce your open-mindedness before reading this book (once you've bought it) by writing the following words on the dotted line across the next page:

"MAYBE HE'S RIGHT"

Thanks,
Bob Etherington

".."

See the previous page

Definitions for Virgins

negotiate (verb) [*nee-**go**-shee-yate*]
1. What you have to do when the other person says "No"
2. What you have to do when desirable assets become scarce

bigdiscounts (noun. pl) [*big-**dis**-cownts*]
What you give when you don't know how to negotiate

paytoomuch (verb) [***pey**-toow-muh-ch*]
What you do if you don't know how to negotiate

Rules for virgin negotiators

1. Nobody will negotiate with you unless they believe you can help them or hurt them.
2. If they keep coming back to the table you have something they want.
3. If you keep coming back to the table they have something you want.

Introduction

You don't start negotiating until the other side says, "No!"

I used to travel a great deal for my job. For this reason I found myself in a camera shop in a Hong Kong shopping mall a few years ago ... I was buying a digital video camera with a friend from the Philippines. The camera was on sale for about USD 2000. Top of the range at that time ... Brand name too.

I went through the time honoured HK ritual with the shopkeeper, "Is that your best price?" The shopkeeper grudgingly knocked off USD 140. I felt good ... $140 off ... whooo! You'd never get that in London! I was about to accept when my friend jumped in. "You must haggle!" she said. (Brazenly ... right there in front of the man ... in front of the whole shop ... in a loud voice too!) "I just did," said I. "Not like that!" she said. "We'll pay $200 that's all," she said to the shopkeeper. "Can't be done!" he said. (Embarrassment.) "Let's go!" she said, and began to walk out. "Just a moment," said the man coming out into the street. "Let's see what we can do."

Ten minutes later we had the camera for $1300 including a carry bag, tripod and a wide-angle lens. We also spent another $700 on an excellent digital still camera selling in London for $1200.

OK, it was actually a "haggle" BUT it was also ... nearly ...very nearly ... a full bodied "successful negotiation". Not a "Hey ... we really screwed 'em!" deal for either side. But then again, nobody walked away feeling "short-changed" either. It was a very good deal for both of us. Leaving the encounter feeling like this, on both sides, is the ideal outcome for a good negotiation. Why do I say this? Because it had many of the elements that mark the difference between basic haggling and sophisticated negotiating:

- It was as wise as it was sensible.
- I would definitely do business there again.
- He would probably be pleased to see me if I went back.
- I would be pleased to go back.

Oh ... no "negotiations" please ... we're from the Northern Hemisphere!

For people who are not originally from Asia, the Middle East or Latin America, real negotiating is not part of our way of life; neither is bargaining or haggling. We Caucasians are, generally, very bad at negotiating. This applies to our home life and work life. It also applies to corporate deals both very small and very large. Many of us are even encouraged to believe it is impolite to embark on a negotiation especially in a "posh" shop or similar intimidating surroundings.

"Can we 'DO' something on the price, Sir? If you need to question the price, Sir, you clearly can't afford it!"

So, with all this built-up angst, agony and vividly imagined future-embarrassment, lurking deep in our genes, we hate even the thought of doing it. We hate the thought so much we are scared to embark on it under any circumstances. We laugh loudly (too loudly?) when we recognize someone very close to home in situations like this ... ourselves:

Harry The Haggler: Now, look. I want twenty for that.

Brian: I – I just gave you twenty.

Harry The Haggler: Now, are you telling me that's not worth twenty shekels?

Brian: No.

Harry The Haggler: Look at it. Feel the quality. That's none of your goat.

Brian: All right. I'll give you nineteen then.

Harry The Haggler: No, no, no. Come on. Do it properly.

Brian: What?

Harry The Haggler: Haggle properly. This isn't worth nineteen.

Brian: Well, you just said it was worth twenty.

Harry The Haggler: Ohh, dear. Ohh, dear. Come on. Haggle.

Brian: Huh. All right. I'll give you ten.

Harry The Haggler: That's more like it. Ten?! Are you trying to insult me?! Me, with a poor dying grandmother?! Ten?!

Brian: All right. I'll give you eleven.

Harry The Haggler: Now you're getting it. Eleven?! Did I hear you right?! Eleven?! This cost me twelve. You want to ruin me?! [...]

Brian: Ohh, tell me what to say. Please!

Harry The Haggler: Offer me fourteen.

Brian: I'll give you fourteen.

Harry The Haggler: He's offering me fourteen for this!
Brian: Fifteen!
Harry The Haggler: Seventeen. My last word. I won't take a penny less, or strike me dead.
Brian: Sixteen.
Harry The Haggler: Done. Nice to do business with you.

From the 1979 Monty Python Film Life Of Brian

So we get "ground to a pulp"

We'll get to the difference between "haggling" (see above) and "negotiating" later, but you get the picture. The upshot of our reluctance to negotiate is that the very few expert negotiators in the Northern Hemisphere who do know how to negotiate, end up painfully screwing us. They don't intend to hurt us but they end up doing so anyway because we don't know how to do it back to them.

Yet people from Asia, the Middle East, Latin America and throughout the second and third worlds in general, are expert at it. We (from the North) vacation in their countries and come back with tales to tell of what happened when we were buying things in the markets, bazaars and "souks". We love the lithe, direct and supple way they do it and secretly we envy them. At the same time we ourselves are afraid to give in to the need to be flexible, inventive and alive to the possibility of the moment. Just like "Brian" when up against "Harry the Haggler" we get frustrated and embarrassed. We are not really able to join them in the expert verbal intercourse. We just want it to be over. And when we come up against them in a serious business transaction they "grind" us again too. It is, for them, a way of life. They have no shame, regret or embarrassment about bargaining, haggling or negotiating. They are brought up to do it from childhood. They expect everybody to do it well too. If you don't engage in it with them (and with gusto) they are somewhat bemused.

So what's in this book for you?

In these pages, as I said before, you will discover the "real" secrets of negotiation ... and you will! In Chapter 1 you will be introduced to the very heart of the issue. And that is that you should only enter in to a negotiation if you really desire (or Aspire) to emerge with a great result. Why? Well, the situation that often makes a negotiation necessary is that you have (or the other side has) already said (or is imminently likely to say) "No" to some standard terms in a proposed transaction. So although many sales training books tell you that such an impasse, deadlock or objection is somehow a "buying signal", taking you closer to deal, there is NO evidence to support this! In fact it is quite the opposite.

The other key reason for investing time in a negotiation is that some resource you want or the other side wants is becoming increasingly scarce and a straight "sale" is not going to provide a satisfactory result. (The current global energy market in which participants are competing for a declining fossil-fuel resource is a prime example.)

If you have tried a classic "sale and purchase transaction" and failed but still want to do business with each other you are now in a more complex situation. You are no longer in a sale; you are on the verge of a "negotiation". And in any negotiation one side has more power than the other. And that word "**power**" needs a little clarification. Because "power" isn't something you're given. Power is omething you take. Power is simply a "feeling".

As a virgin negotiator if you feel, at this "imminent negotiation" stage, that you are in a weak position or you are at all half-hearted about it, then all the evidence (and there is a great deal of research to support this) points to "not such a great final outcome" for you. As with so much of success in business and negotiation (and life in general) it comes down to your Attitude and your Aspiration. So in Chapter 1 we will discuss what you can do to raise these before you begin. Once you have flown through Chapter 1 you will be ready for the next big secret revealed in Chapter 2 ... the alternative landing site (or "letter in your back pocket"). The confidence you gain from knowing that you have previously planned somewhere to set yourself down if the original journey doesn't go according to plan is enormous. All virgin negotiators need to learn the essential nature that prior planned options give them. In many international companies the presentation to the Board or Executive Committee of such a back-up plan, is now mandated before the senior management permit any team to sit down across the negotiating table with a counterparty. If it's good enough for them it must be good enough for you.

In Chapter 3, I will ensure that you understand the difference between selling, haggling and negotiating. I will do that by illustrating the clear differences. You will see that "haggling", in particular, is largely a financial trimming and bartering issue, whilst selling and negotiating are, or should be, focused on perceived value. Negotiating is the "poor cousin" of selling. You will discover that you should always endeavour to "sell" the other side before you get into a negotiation. In "selling" you and the other party agree a deal and price around a set of standard pre-set terms. The pricing may be affected by a price discounting formula, which is a part of these standard terms. The terms are either your own or the other party's or a mixture of the two.

When it comes to "negotiating" a complication has set in. A deal on standard terms has not been possible, so you must be prepared to vary the terms in some way. The "virgin" in the negotiating arena generally attempts to get the deal "closed" by varying just one "term": the price! And it's usually by reducing it if you're the seller or paying too much if you're the buyer. I have lost track of the number of times I have heard from sellers: "It's the price ... we're just too expensive!" Or from buyers: "It's no good ... we have to pay their price ... there's nothing else we can do!" The truth is, in fact, that quite a few things come before price, as you will see in Chapter 3. This book is about negotiating not haggling.

Chapter 4 is entitled "Deconstructing the 'No'". We've all heard smart-asses reeling out the put-down epithet: "What part of 'No' don't you understand?" And yet there are generally many factors which have lead to "No", whether it's our side saying "No" or the other side saying "No". As a "virgin" you absolutely need to sit down and analyse why you're really saying "No". What do you really want from this negotiation? If you sincerely believe that it's the money you want, what do you want to do with it? Is there some other way you could achieve the same result? Why do you want it? OK and why do you want that? Boil it down ... then boil it down again.

If you want a parallel example it is similar to analysing the folklore relationship between employers and employees. Between these two parties there is generally a view, on the "employer" side that the "number one" issue for employees is "money". Yet when asked, employees rarely rate money as "number one". So in the same way you must analyse all your needs prior to entering into the negotiation and then mentally place yourself in the shoes of the other side. What's behind their "No"?

It is rarely "just the money". Chapter 4 shows you how to do this and provides you with a planning tool to make it easier.

Then in Chapter 5 we finally get round to what is often for many humans the BIG one ... the people problem. "He makes me so mad!" "I am sick and tired of the way that woman behaves!" "Those people! That Asian guy at the end of the table never said a word!" "I thought that British man would never stop talking." "I just can't negotiate with the Russians ... it's their attitude." "And in the middle of the meeting this Arab's uncle suddenly showed up and everything ground to a halt ... it was just stupid. I'm not doing that again." "I don't understand how those Americans could even consider negotiating ... it was the first time we'd met. I don't even know them!"

Human beings often don't like each other for a number of reasons. These are sometimes to do with perceptions gained from the TV and what they read in the newspapers. Occasionally and irrationally they pile a particular ethnic group together and decide not to like them. Often it is because of the influence of local political propaganda. I was recently asked by an American immigration officer at Houston International Airport, who noticed a couple of Iranian stamps in my British passport, "Why do the Iranians all hate us?" Yet "hate" is hardly the feeling you get walking the streets of Tehran in the early 21st century; a city in which most of the well-educated young majority would do anything to learn American English and travel to the USA.

The reality is that most people in the World simply want to have a nice life. They see the world through their own spectacles and not ours. They are not against you and me ... they are simply for themselves. Just because they don't look, sound, behave and think like people from my family, company, ethnic group, or country, doesn't mean that either you or I cannot negotiate with them. I may not like them or you (and vice versa) for many reasons both rational and irrational. But if there's mutually advantageous business to be done I will set these reasons aside and using the techniques described in Chapter 5 negotiate with you until we "do" the deal.

Machiavellian, manipulative, mind gaming, psychological tricks ... this is what you'll find in Chapter 6. Well ... OK, not quite as bad as that but it would be remiss of me in an instructional book about negotiating (and specifically written for virgin negotiators) not to outline some of the simple well researched psychological tools that can be used to persuade another human brain to your way of thinking. You don't have to use them if you don't want to but you DO need to recognize if they are being used as "ploys" against you. They are very well researched but not at all complex. In fact, they are so simple that most people's prior reaction to every single one is, "That would NEVER work against me!" And yet if, during a negotiating training class, I don't warn the delegates that I am about to use one of the tools to influence their behaviour and subsequently get them, unconsciously, to do something they would not have done otherwise (for example to give me a completely undeserved round of applause for something), most people are profoundly shocked. They often apologize after the session for being so unguarded. No need to apologize. We are all surprisingly susceptible to very simple ploys of people who would like to do business with us.

So the first six chapters in this book explain the planning tools and techniques (OK ... sometimes even "ploys") available to and used by all experienced and successful negotiators. Then we come to "field-application", because Chapter 7 is about the way you behave when confronted by your real life negotiating counterparty. "Be on your best behaviour" was an instruction that ruled my childhood. But for a negotiator much academic research over the past 40 years or so has shown that there are a few clearly identifiable behavioural habits which can either wreck or make a great negotiation. In Chapter 7 you will learn that there is no autopilot in negotiating. There is no formulaic approach which will get you to the landing field of your choice every time without further real-time input from you. It is time to introduce you to the classic bad-behaviours which average negotiators regularly trip over and fall into and the counter good-behaviours employed habitually by successful, experienced negotiators. Chapter 7 reveals four of these on each side of the fence. Four good ones as used by great negotiators and four common accidental "wreckers" mistakenly used by average negotiators.

Finally, Chapter 8 brings everything together and shows you how to prepare and plan for a real negotiation, using everything previously covered in the book. And, as you will see as you get in to the book, it ends as it begins. Negotiation is generally not a thing that happens and then ends and then a new one starts again ... it is a continuous process. The reason we are very often prepared to negotiate in the first place is that we want to deal with these people again so we invest time and effort to give them a little and take something back for ourselves in return. Once you have all these relatively simple skills buttoned down you will be all set for your next real negotiation.

Great Negotiating Skills is not a long book and it doesn't need to be. As a topic "negotiating" can be dressed up in a lot of superfluous detail (in order to get you to pay more or buy another book?). Or you can apply just the techniques in these eight chapters and see what happens.

So there's the challenge. Just go and do what I describe in these pages. Nothing else is needed. First make sure you really aspire to come out of your next negotiation with a great result ... nothing else is more important than this. Then: 1. Be properly prepared (most negotiators are not). 2. Know clearly what you're going to do if it doesn't work out (most negotiators have no such Plan B). 3. Never make a statement when you could ask a question (most negotiators don't realize how they mess up by "telling" too much). 4. Control their perception of time (most negotiators have no idea how to do this or how valuable it is). 5. Control their perception of your power (most negotiators have no idea that power has little to do with reality and nearly everything to do with perception).

Then, after your next negotiation, when you have applied these lessons, drop me a line (my address is at the end of the book) and let me know what happened ... good or not so good ... I'm not a shrinking violet I can take it.

That's it.

I look forward to hearing about your success!

SECTION 1

The elevator to success is out of order. You'll
have to use the stairs, one step at a time.

JOE GIRARD, WORLD'S GREATEST SALESMAN
(GUINNESS BOOK OF WORLD RECORDS)

Aspiration and Attitude

"At heart we underestimate ourselves. We do not really believe in ourselves and remain for that reason weak, ineffectual, even impotent, when we could be strong, dominant, victorious."

DR NORMAN VINCENT PEALE

So you want to be a successful negotiator. That is a very good starting point. It is a lot better than wanting to be a failure.

But how good you actually are at negotiating depends on a little bit more than a "want". In this book I will show you many techniques of persuasion and "value creation". But how good you actually become as a negotiator depends on one important factor more than anything else. And it is one factor that most similar books ignore: your *aspiration*.

First ... Who am I?

My name is Bob Etherington and I am a salesman.

I know that is similar to the introduction given by people in an Alcoholics Anonymous meeting but, judging by results, I am an experienced and successful communicator, business persuader and sales manager. It has taken me over 37 years in the "school of hard knocks" to get there but I've made it. (Hurrah!) For the record I am also a pilot, an engineer and a business owner, but selling activities still take up most of my business day.

So I'm about to save you 37 years of toil by condensing a big chunk of that knowledge into about 37,000 words in the little book you are now holding. I am not better than you, but I have learnt a lot about persuasion in business and that's what you'll find in this book.

Even though many business people are not very keen on either *selling* things or *negotiating* deals, it is a fact that for just about all commercial enterprises, there is nothing more important than those two activities. Why? Because without them nothing else happens.

Now, when you're learning to *sell*, (I was initially trained by Rank Xerox in the UK c.1970) one of the required classes usually covers how to make initial contact with prospective customers. One method I was taught was how to write effective, door-opening, sales letters. "Lesson 1" on this subject included some explanation of the way most intended recipients tend to read sales letters.

You see, once your prospective customers have been enticed to open the envelope (getting them to do that is an art and science all on its own) they tend to do something unexpected. They look at the *end* of the letter first.

That is why most effective sales letters always have a "P.S." at the end. And the strongest sales message in the letter is always contained in that "P.S.". But as this is a *book* about negotiating and not a letter, it has a P.S. (Pre Script) at the beginning and a P.S. (Post Script) at the end and they are both the same.

Because my most important message for you (a negotiating virgin) is contained in those P.S.s and it is key to your success as a top negotiator.

Here it is:

P.S. Never enter into a negotiation unless you aspire to emerge from it with the very best possible deal you can imagine.

As with so many areas of life, research and academic observation proves, over and over again, that successfully negotiated outcomes usually have little to do with either training, knowledge or experience. They DO always have a lot to do with your Attitude and Aspiration.

I have attended and conducted many negotiating training programmes around the world in the past few years. Delegates are often able to pass various assessment tests at the end of their programmes. They know, off-by-heart, the supposed formulae for conducting a perfect technical negotiation.They play the business-games and simulated negotiation exercises perfectly. Yet put them in the field in a real negotiation involving real assets, real products, real services and very real money and they fail to win the deals they could have won for themselves or their businesses.

I have been introduced to people who are supposed to be their company's "top negotiator" with several years experience. They have invited me to observe them in action and give feedback. [*What people usually want in these cases is the positive feedback ... in other words the good stuff only to bolster their fragile egos. Nothing at all, despite the initial brief, is really required from me, as their consultant, on the not-so-good side.*] I have then sat at the back and watched the action. What happens is that this expert often conducts it technically, in a reasonably average manner. Indeed, he (or she) often gets a deal agreed, as if a "deal-at-any-cost" was the original objective. Yet the other side, often younger and hence by default with less experience, but with greater hunger and aspiration, gets easily the best cut of the negotiation.

On one occasion I was asked to watch, listen and observe one of these top "experienced negotiators" negotiate for my edification. (He was actually my boss at the time). He finally became so frustrated with his lack of progress and yet determined to impress (me?) that he eventually uttered the immortal words to the leader of the other team, "Is there any other financial incentive I can offer you to get you to give us the deal today?" The other side's eyes spun like the reels in a fruit machine. I'm surprised their leader didn't mime a cash register and say, "Cha-Ching!"

How much or how badly you desire and aspire to achieve the best negotiated outcome, compared with the same desire and aspiration on the other side of the table, is key to leaving the negotiating table with the best deal for you.

It isn't a case of reaching a "great deal" at the expense of the other side. It is simply realizing your own value and thinking and acting in a manner that conveys this sense of purpose and confidence to the people sitting across the table from you. It is even possible to extend this idea to a team of people who are negotiating on your behalf by confidently setting an expectation of a great result.

In some of the in-house negotiation training programmes that I run for companies, we actually prove the validity of this high expectation/aspiration approach by being a little underhand with one of our training exercises.

We set up the delegates in two *almost* identical parallel negotiation exercises in separate rooms. The asset they negotiate over has no tangible value either to the buyer or the seller ... it is all in their perception.

The buying side in both negotiation groups has an identical briefing sheet. The sellers, on the other hand, are each set different objectives. One "selling" team is set an objective to get £50,000 for the asset. The other "selling" team just £20,000. What happens, every time we set the exercise, is that the team we settle the higher expectation on initially ends up negotiating a much higher final price for their asset. The amazing thing is that the buyers don't feel hard done by and the sellers don't feel imposed on either. The teams are generally shocked at the large difference between the outcomes and the reason for it, when this is revealed to them at the end.

If we set ourselves high standards and goals and truly aspire and expect to reach them it is amazing what we can achieve. In his book *The Luck Factor* (an academic examination of the repeatable behaviours of lucky people) Professor Richard Wiseman of the University of Hertfordshire, UK has found that one of the four key behaviours of lucky people is that they expect to be lucky. So prior to negotiating, a key behaviour for you *virgin negotiators* to work on is your level of aspiration and expectation.

This isn't always easy ... as the 19th century American philosopher Henry David Thoreau said: "Most men live lives of quiet desperation and go to the grave with the song still in them", and it seems to me, despite the mountains of positive-thinking self-help books which are available, not much has changed in the 21st century. (Are we really hardwired to feel so inferior to each other?)

Just a few years ago an anonymous survey taken in the First Class section of a major airline revealed that 76% of people seated up there "in-the-nose" believed that they did not deserve to be there! They thought that sooner or later someone would discover that they were not worthy. That their value was much less than they had been leading other people to believe.

Yet most people I meet have the potential to become anything they want to become.

In a previous book (*Presentation Skills for Quivering Wrecks*) I said that in my experience most business people around the world seem to be playing a cassette-tape/CD in their heads which isn't helping them at all. The message that's playing over and over again is: "What will they do when they discover I'm only me?"

Virgin Negotiators! ... if this is you it must stop. Today. Stop listening to that tape.

Our aspirations as human beings are very much dictated by our own self esteem. And our self esteem comes mainly from the constant conversations going on in our head.

I am actually typing this part of the book, in August 2007, seated upstairs on a 747 "Jumbo" on my way back to London from leading an in-house negotiation workshop for a company in Asia. [*Thinks: "I see from the moving map display on the seat-back TV in front of me that we are currently flying just north of Istanbul ... there are some great natural carpet negotiators just below me."*]

Anyway, on the particular Asian training programme I have just delivered, there was a very able delegate – an Australian – who proved that he is, potentially, a very good technical negotiator. The problem has been, all week, that he has showed little belief in himself. He has constantly refaced every exercise with an excuse:

"No but ... I just want to warn you I'll be no good at this." (He was great.)

"No but ... I'm actually a 'techie' I haven't got the experience in the sales area." (He was fine.)

"No but ... our product IS far too expensive." (No it isn't.)

"No but ... in the *real* world we have to give our customers a discount ... they demand it." (I'm sure they do. Price is *always* an objection – but you're not going to give them one.)

When it came to personal aspiration the Australian was shooting himself in the foot at every turn. If he continues like this he will continue to give away value to counterparties, which they would otherwise be quite willing to pay for.

By changing his in-head conversation first he will very rapidly – surprisingly rapidly – alter his perception of himself and subsequently other people's perception of him.

As a starter I suggested swapping the "No but ..." (which he usually begins every sentence with) for "Yes and ..." thus removing all the negative parts of the following sentence. If he concentrates on this, I estimate other people will see the change in him in about two weeks.

When my business partner and I first set up our training business, on the dining table in my London apartment a few years ago, we never once told a lie about our size or the startup nature of our business. It simply never arose as a question from any potential customer and as they didn't ask, we didn't say anything. They told us the types of problem they wanted solved ... we told them how we could help and they, more often than not, engaged us. Sometimes before they knew our fee. We always thought and acted as if we were part of a huge organization which, until we set up on our own, is exactly the type of organization we had been working in.

Our aspiration level was high. We offered and delivered a high level of service so there were no complaints. We even appointed an external chairman for our company who would set a constant expectation of high performance and sales targets if we should ever falter in our resolve. Our strategy worked so well that we started to gain some really large international clients. After a few assignments our main contact from one particular large client bumped into me one day at London Heathrow airport.

"Hi Bob," he said. "I was in your street, at that tennis shop, earlier today. Your offices are near there aren't they? I didn't see your office block. Where is it?" (Office block? ... Office block? It was the two of us with one phone and one (borrowed) laptop at my dining room table!)

But our aspiration levels were high as were our expectations. When negotiating deals for ourselves we never once gave in to the discount pressure ... we didn't have to. We always appeared to be busy ... we kept ourselves "scarce". We held our nerve when we were up against competitors even when our diary was empty! We "walked away" from the negotiating table a number of times whenever our fees *were* under pressure. It was odd how often on those occasions the assignments and the money chased us ... about 80% of the time as it happens. A typical illustration of this is shown in a client's email copied word for word below:

Dear Bob,

Thank you for a series of interesting discussions over the past two months with respect to our proposed sales and marketing programme. We have just completed our monthly board meeting during which we considered your proposal in parallel with those from your competitors. I have to tell you that your fees are very high by comparison and this was the view of the whole board. Nevertheless we accept your proposal at the rates quoted and request that you let us know as soon as possible when you can start the work.

John

So can any of us tap into some psychological tools which will increase our individual self esteem, expectation and aspiration to a level which will bring us up to "top-negotiator" standard? Yes ... and the answer is instantly to hand: modern sports-psychology ... the world of techniques to which footballer David Beckham, golfer Tiger Woods, the whole of the 2006/7 Australian Cricket team (and just about all successful sports stars) attribute their long standing and continuing success.

You see most top sports stars are only human. They are not looking for success in a bottle of the ubiquitously named "banned-substance". They know they have to find it in themselves. They suffer from all the self doubt and lack of self belief that you do. I know you never admit it and that with your friends and family, just like those sports stars (and the First Class passengers in that Boeing 747), you talk a good *public* talk. But left to their own devices, most people's self-talk chatter is putting them down instead of up.

One of the most often faced challenges experienced by sports stars is how to improve their performance. They are frustrated that they *know* they often possess superior, physical attributes and strengths compared with their competitors (probably just like you and the things you would like to negotiate with a counterparty) and yet they're consistently being out performed by their competition (like you are probably being out-negotiated by the team on the other side of the table).

In so many of these sports cases the one thing that separates their final performance from that of the others in the race has been found to be based in their belief as to their ability to outperform the competition. Simply put they are operating with a limiting belief as to their strengths and abilities compared with those on the other side. However research shows that an individual's *core beliefs* in any given area of their life will ultimately determine the reality they draw into their life! ... Top performer, Poor performer or Average performer.

So how do you go about changing a limiting belief to a positive one – one that will result in a transformation of your expectations and aspirations? One that will bring about your transformation from an average negotiator to a top negotiator?

First, can I ask you ... do you talk to yourself? (*Do I? ... I don't know? Let me see now ...*) You see it has long been established by psychologists and neuroscientists that we all (every person in the world) carry on a continuous dialogue, or self-talk, of something between 150 and 300 words each minute. This means that we process between 45,000 and 50,000 thoughts each day. Most of this dialogue is harmless and serves our daily activities such as, "I need to stop at the supermarket". The problem comes about when your inner dialogue takes on a negative connotation like, "I'll have to give them a discount ... they are in a much stronger position than us". "We are only a start-up in this market. We don't have the experience to compete at this level." Or, "There are so many companies similar to us. We don't stand a chance of getting it." The constant negative reinforcement created by our habitual negative self-talk results directly in the creation of a limiting belief (or beliefs) that go on to become self-fulfilling prophecies.

A belief – positive or negative – is a feeling of certainty. Beliefs are, literally, hard-wired into our brain in comfortable grooves or neural motorways. Incoming data from your senses travel on these neural motorways on the way to interpretation in the brain. Therefore, if you sincerely want to change an unresourceful/limiting belief into a totally empowering belief, you must divert the negative neural motorway created in your brain.

You can achieve this in exactly the same way that the roadways were laid down in the first place: by using self-talk, or what are generally called "affirmations". Affirmations are statements of fact or belief (negative or positive) that will ultimately lead to the end result you expect. Words that follow the phrase, "I am", such as "I am a great negotiator" or "I am confident in the value of my service" are an affirmation. The simplicity of affirmations often makes more cynical people dismiss them. But ask any successful person for an opinion (and I often do) and you will hear no cynicism. Affirmations are regularly used by successful business people and professional athletes.

This is how you can compose effective affirmations for yourself. The process is a simple one. First, identify the areas of your life which are not working to your satisfaction ... in your case the area of successful negotiation. Now, write out your aspirational affirmations that represent things the way you want them to be. These will be the vehicles for creating new resourceful/positive motorways. Your affirmation should be short and to the point. It must be so simple that a small child will understand it. And because your brain cannot hold a negative thought it must always be stated in the positive. "I am a truly confident negotiator" not "I am not worried about negotiating." Also, your affirmation must be stated in the present tense – as if it has already happened, for example, "I am a strong successful negotiator".

Now you are going to use these affirmations to play a trick on your brain and to alter your perception of yourself and the world.

You think your perception (the way you see things) is reality and that it can't be changed? I'm afraid you're wrong and I am about to prove it. Before you go any further let me prove to you that your brain plays tricks on you all the time. With these aspirations you will just start getting your own back. Below is a chessboard. Two of the squares are marked respectively "A" and "B". Here's the question: which is the darker square "A" or "B"?

Reality? Out there ... or ... just in your head?

Take your time ... it's easy isn't it? Of course square "A" is darker ... of course it is ... any fool can see that! But what if I were to tell you something. What if I were to tell you that they are both identical shades of grey! What if I were to tell you they are EXACTLY the same colour! Look again ... OK, now you think I'm totally crazy! But they are the same. It is just that your eye, seeing a three dimensional picture, tells your brain that things towards the background get darker and things in the foreground are lighter so that is what you perceive ... it just isn't reality. This illusion was compiled by the psychologist Edward H. Adelson at MIT in Boston and to check that we are both not "bonkers", go to his website: **http :/ / web.mit.edu /persci /people/ adelson/checkershadow_illusion.html** where you can check and prove it for yourself. (And yes ... as you will see, just like the squares above, they are exactly the same shade of grey.)

So now you are going start presenting different images and self-talk to your brain in order to change its perception of reality in exactly the same way. You are going to change your perception of reality until, like the chessboard squares, it becomes your reality!

So are you ready to apply this science? (Remember this technique is effective in all areas of human performance ... not just aspirational negotiation.)

Sit upright on your bed or in a comfortable chair. Shut your eyes and take two minutes or so to relax progressively from toes to head. Imagine you are at the top of a 100-step staircase and mentally find yourself walking down, counting off the steps as you go. 100 ... 99 ... 98 ... 97 ... at each step feel yourself becoming more and more relaxed. At the bottom of the imaginary staircase speak your affirmation aloud between five to twenty times. (This depends on the time you have and the number of beliefs you are reprogramming.) When you have completed this exercise bring yourself out of your relaxed state, slowly from toes to head, and open your eyes.

Repeat this every day for just 30 days and see the difference in yourself. Remember all you have to do is "do it". The change will start in your brain long before you are conscious of the change.

Why do you have to "say" the affirmation out loud? By speaking your affirmation aloud you are involving more of your brain by including two more of your senses: hearing and feeling. You must trust this process. You must give your affirmations a chance to achieve your desired outcome. If you worry or doubt yourself or wonder if your affirmations are working, you will convey this worry to your subconscious mind. And in doing that you will generate the belief that your desire may not come to pass or the affirmation may not succeed. This process works for everyone who does it. Just do it.

It is your beliefs that produce your life experiences, not the other way around. Organize and control your beliefs using affirmations to create a life filled with successful experiences.

These experiences will reinforce the beliefs that created them. The business world is not necessarily led by the best people. It is always led by the people who *think* they're the best.

All the available research shows that when experience and training are pitted against high aspiration and high expectation those aspirational negotiators tend to come out on top more often.

It is that simple.

SECTION 2

Question: What is Plan B?
Answer: Not Plan A

"There is nothing worth less to a pilot than altitude above you or runway behind you. Take-offs are optional ... Landings are compulsory. So what's your plan?"

DAVE LAWRENCE, MY FIRST FLYING INSTRUCTOR

Learning to fly a plane is great fun ... I did it ... it's not difficult ... 12–15 hours to "first solo" for averagely intelligent people. So why does it take a minimum of 50 or 60 hours ... or even more, for most people to get a full flying licence? It is the time taken mostly in training the novice what to do if something DOES go, unexpectedly, not-according-to plan. Before a pilot sets out on a flight he must first plan his route and, most important of all, where he will land if he has to come down early or unexpectedly. Every couple of years, in order to maintain your UK flying licence, you have to go up with an instructor or examiner who at any moment will pull back on the throttle levers high over the English countryside and say, "You've just had an engine failure. Where are you going to land?" and expect you to select a site and glide the "engineless" lump of metal down to within a few hundred feet of your designated pre-planned spot before mercifully applying full power again. Or they will get you to wear a pair of blacked-out spectacles ("Foggles") and fly you around for several minutes in order to disorient you before allowing you to remove the glasses. At which point they will ask you to identify your exact location and then take them to the nearest alternative airfield. Bursting into tears won't hack it ... you must have a pre-prepared plan!

Understanding the huge power and confidence you give yourself at the negotiating table when you start out with an alternative landing site in mind (for use if something should go wrong) is very important. In negotiating I always ask virgin negotiators think of it as a letter in your back pocket (LIYBP). When I was an employee I always negotiated better salary increases for myself if I had an offer letter from another employer in my trouser pocket. I rarely had to mention it ... my confidence said it all. And the "letter-in-your-backpocket" idea is critical to your elevation from Virgin Negotiator to Top Negotiator. This is because it provides you with the confidence to act in a more courageous manner. You will always make a wiser decision about whether to accept a negotiated agreement if you have previously established what your alternative is (or alternatives are).

In simple terms, if your negotiated agreement is better than the contents of the LIYBP, then you should accept it. If the agreement reached so far, is not better than the contents of your LIYBP, then you should continue to negotiate until you reach a better agreement. If you cannot, then discontinue the negotiation. You would be surprised how often people emerge from the negotiating table with a deal a long way from their original intention. They lose sight of the objective in the excitement of the moment. Any deal rather than the right deal becomes the objective.

You think it can't happen? That of course you wouldn't lose sight of your primary objective? I have to challenge that thought.

There is an exercise we give to corporate negotiation workshops consisting of highly qualified, experienced and well educated 21st century executives which illustrates how easy it is to quickly lose sight of what a wise agreement would look like.

It goes like this: I produce from my wallet a genuine $50 bill (US Dollars). I tell the class that it is up for auction in 50 cent increments. The winner will receive the note. Anyone in the room can bid for it in sequence (I tell them I will go round the class clockwise). Anyone can drop out at any time but cannot then rejoin the auction. We open the bidding.

After the first two bids I suddenly remember that there is one auction rule I have omitted ... the second-best bid, at the end, also has to pay up. A couple of sensible people immediately drop out but for the rest greed and fear blind them to what's happening. In particular nobody in the room now wants to lose and as the number of participants slowly reduces, "not coming second" becomes the dominant objective. So powerful is this desire that during the exercise, we regularly find the bidding for the $50 bill not only reaches but exceeds the face value. It is not uncommon to find three or four people bidding $53 ... $53.50 ... $54 ... $54.50 ... for a $50 bill. It is atthis stage that I bring the auction to a sensible (and wise) conclusion. I point out how easy it is for any of us to become caught up in the proceedings and end up with a deal that makes no sense for our side at all.

So a previously established LIYBP keeps you focused and stops you agreeing to something stupid.

If you cannot negotiate a better agreement for your side (or for yourself), then you must consider concluding the negotiations and exercising your alternative. In the real world the costs of doing that must be considered as well but, as the saying goes, "When you're up to your backside in alligators it is difficult to remind yourself that your objective was to drain the swamp!" In essence your LIYBP will protect you both from prematurely agreeing to terms that are unfavourable for you and from saying "no" to terms it would actually be in your interest to accept.

Having a great LIYBP increases your negotiating power. Because, if you can improve the contents of your LIYBP, you will increase your *actual* negotiating power and the *perception* of your negotiating power at the same time. We humans are always communicating; it is not something we control particularly well. Over 55% of human communication is picked up by other people from our unconscious body language and another 38% from our tone of voice. So good negotiators "feel" when their opponent is desperate for an agreement. They can "feel" that there is no Plan B on the other side. When this happens they will demand much more from you and you will have to capitulate. On the other hand if you do appear to have many options, outside the negotiation, then you are likely to get many more concessions from your counterparty in an effort to keep you at the negotiating table.

So what happens when the reality is that the other side does have more power? What happens when the "Letter In Your Back Pocket" is not as good as you would like? When, like many small business owners trying to sell to a large corporation, you are an unknown entity? When the other side is, more or less, saying: "I don't know who you are or what you think you can offer us, or how you rank against our regular supplier but ... well, you're here now so let's negotiate!"

The truth is that even when an effective negotiator (or negotiating team) does not have good options outside the negotiation, they often *think* they do and this is what makes the difference (see Chapter 1!). For example, both sides may *think* that they can get the deal they want (the big company negotiators *think* they can grind a price discount out of the smaller company or go elsewhere ... the smaller company thinks they can persuade the larger one that their offering is unique). Yet, because most buying decisions are made at a deeply unconscious level, perceptions are the biggest issue when it comes to deciding whether or not to accept an agreement. If a top, "aspirational" negotiator thinks that they have a great LIYBP, even when the reality is that they are actually weak, they will, very often, pursue that option, even if it is not as good as they think it is.

Even when your LIYBP contains (as mine has in the past) things like: *If I can't get this deal I will vacation for the summer and write a book; I have ten other prospective customers in various stages of the sales process ... one of them will drop ... if this particular one fails it isn't the end of the world; there are at least five other businesses I could begin in less than a week* ... then it is very spooky how often the business has chased me. Yet when I have convinced myself that a particular assignment is mine for the taking and I have no LIYBP then I am often "surprised" by my failure to get it: "We felt the other company had a better understanding of our issues and culture."

At the end of his life Sir Winston Churchill said he felt like an aeroplane at the end of its journey, nearly out of fuel, searching for a safe landing field. That was OK in the mid 20th century, but as a successful 21st century negotiator you shouldn't even be preparing to take-off without knowing where your safe alternative landing field will be.

One of the great and well-publicized LIYBP success stories in the past few years in London, UK was over the threatened increase in land rental demanded by the owners of the land on which the London Eye stands. The owners of this "bigwheel" tourist attraction had been paying £65,000 per year in rental. In 2005 the owners of the land, represented by a powerful London businessman Lord Hollick, gave them notice to quit unless the London Eye's owners increased their rental to £2,500,000 per year ... a whopping 3880% increase!

Extreme opening positions for a negotiation? Certainly! On one side a strong and successful business owner and on the other the cash-strapped, debt laden owners of a popular tourist attraction. What did the London Eye's owners do for a LIYBP? They appealed to London's Mayor, Ken Livingston who gave them a great one: *a threatened compulsory purchase order to be placed on the land by the Corporation of London!*

The resulting negotiation concluded in February 2006 left all sides happy. With the threat of the compulsory purchase order known to be in the attraction-owner's back pocket, the owners of the land negotiated a deal which gave them just one-fifth of their originally demanded rental: £500,000 ... an increase? Yes but not nearly as much as they had originally hoped for. But, on the other hand, guaranteed for "the foreseeable future"... (and as all business people know there is no such thing as a "bad" profit). Also in the course of the negotiations the original owners of the "Eye" agreed to sell all their shares to the waxworks pioneers "Madame Tussauds" and so rid themselves of all their debt.

So in most of the ways that we have to measure a successful negotiation it was successful. Each party could walk away with something more than they might have had if they had become totally intransigent. But without the effective LIYBP what would have happened? And if Lord Hollick representing the landowners, had read this book first would he have established an even more powerful LIYBP of his own? We shall never know.

I care ... I really care ... (but not that much)

Herb Cohen, American Negotiator And Trainer

The top American negotiator, Herb Cohen has said that negotiating is "the game of life" and each negotiation should be treated like a competitive game. Because, according to Herb, when it comes to the outcome a game is where: "You care! ... you really care! ... (but not that much!)"

The more you can negotiate and at the same time treat it like a game the better the outcome will tend to be for you. Unfortunately the more personally and emotionally involved you become (e.g. when you're negotiating on behalf of yourself) the more inept you become; the more the other side will pick up your anxiety and the less likely it is that the outcome will go your way.

It would be preferable if it were the other way round. It would be better if we could all be more successful with our "personal" negotiations than in our negotiations on behalf of other people. Alas it just isn't so.

Because if, like Herb, you actually earn a living negotiating on behalf of other companies (in his case preferably large multinationals and rich entrepreneurs) and get rewarded with a tiny ercentage of the huge value of any successful deal, you tend to do better for them because you don't really know the people employing you. In other words when it comes to your human attachment to them, you "care ... (*but not that much!*)".

But, reader, you're a "virgin negotiator" (which is why you're reading this book) and that, in turn, means that whereas you MAY one day be able to earn part of your living negotiating for other people, you WILL, doubtless quite soon, be personally involved with the outcome of negotiations for yourself. This is where the Letter in

Your Back Pocket (LIYBP) concept will provide an enormous boost in your confidence and enable you to "play the game".

When I started consciously applying this concept to my own personal negotiations (property, jobs, automobiles) in about 1979, I found that I was able and willing to take more risks ... to hold out for what I wanted. And it was amazing how the outcomes of such confident negotiation were more and more in my favour.

BUT BEWARE

Beware ... I am not perfect. Don't do as I do ... do as I say!

When I recently treated myself to an expensive car I ignored my own methods! I walked into the negotiation with no LIYBP. I was too clever by half! As a result I became emotionally involved with the process. I became too serious. It was no longer a game. I cared, I really cared ... I really DID.

It became life or death!

The car was the right colour ... the right model ... the right spec ... the right wheels ... the perfect everything!

I became inept!

As a result I paid too much ... I know I paid too much. I could have negotiated a great deal with a little more preparation. I could have sent my brother in to negotiate. He doesn't care about cars like I do. He would have treated it like a game.

Don't misunderstand me I do like the car but laziness and arrogance got in my way.

You and I need to prepare our LIYBPs every time so that we "care ... really care ... (but not that much!)".

So how can you, a "virgin negotiator", set about deciding on the contents of the LIYBP for your next negotiation? Start by answering these simple questions:

- Why do you want to negotiate?
- Why should the other side negotiate with you?
- How can you help or harm them?
- How can they help or harm you?
- What will you do if the negotiation doesn't work out?
- What do you think they will do if the negotiation does not work out? If I had been more patient with myself over "that car" (see above) I would have prepared my LIYBP something like this:

WHY DO I WANT TO NEGOTIATE?

Because I want this particular make and model of car on the very best terms I can get. It is an expensive purchase, even second-hand, and spending time on the negotiation could save me between £5000 and £8000 on the deal.

WHY SHOULD THE OTHER SIDE NEGOTIATE WITH ME?

Because car sales are slow during this – holiday – time of year. Because there are plenty of cars for sale in the UK at the moment, it is a buyers market. Because, relatively speaking, there are not really many people who can afford to buy an expensive motor vehicle. Because there are plenty of other dealers I can go to if this particular dealer won't negotiate.

HOW CAN I HELP THEM OR HARM THEM?

I can help them by buying the car quickly with no need for a "trade-in". I can help the salesman reach his monthly target (he is bound to have one and a sales-manager breathing down his neck). I can harm the salesman by walking away and taking my money (and his commission) somewhere else. I can tell other potential customers about their intransigent attitude.

HOW CAN THEY HELP OR HARM ME?

They can help me by agreeing to a good price. They can help me by offering a good credit deal. They can help me by including an extended warranty. They can harm me by refusing a deal so that I have to go on a hunt for other dealers around London.

WHAT WILL I DO IF IT DOESN'T WORK OUT?

I will go to another dealer. Or, I will buy privately and get the car inspected before purchase by one of the motoring organizations. Or, I will save the money by not buying a car at all. I don't NEED a car in London so I will invest the funds instead.

WHAT WILL THEY DO IF IT DOESN'T WORK OUT?

Sit in their large expensive showroom and "hope" another prospect with a thick wallet stops by. Cold-call some of their past customers to try and get them interested. Call me up later and try to entice me with a better offer.

It isn't difficult ... but feeling confident about your previously thought-through alternative landing sites will pay you back handsomely!

You need to write these things down ... writing makes ideas become concrete.

You should make sure that your list of alternative possible actions (if this negotiation does not work out) is a practical one and not just pie-in-the-sky.

You will find it beneficial to also consider the LIYBP options of the other side before you enter the negotiation. Later you will be working on ways to weaken the other side's alternative options during the negotiation.

SECTION 3

Haggle Haggle ...
Barter Barter ... Sell Sell ...
"Negotiate"

"You gotta to know when to hold them ...
know when to fold them ... know when to
walk away ... know when to run. You never
count your money when you're seated at the
table ... there'll be time enough for counting
when the dealing's done!"

KENNY ROGERS,
US COUNTRY AND WESTERN SINGER
– "THE GAMBLER"

Now STOP!

Do NOT negotiate!

Step away from the Negotiating Table!

Before we go any further with this book I am going to make a request:

Please don't waste your time "negotiating" until you have first tried to "sell" your proposition to the other side. Selling done "properly" as a technique, is much easier and quicker than negotiating.

In short "negotiating" is the poor-cousin of "selling".

No apologies if you DO see yourself as a great "Negotiat-OR". Because, the truth is, you simply don't have to "negotiate" if the other side has more or less accepted, without argument, the basic terms you have presented. If they accept and agree your standard terms, and you agree theirs, it's a successful "sale".

It takes a lot less time to simply "sell" or "buy" a product, service or idea. And, as time is money, it is a lot less costly to sell rather than negotiate. So, your first objective should always be a straightforward sale or purchase.

If, on the other hand, the other side would clearly like to work with you (or you with them) but there is a need for either you or them to significantly vary the terms in some way, then you are on the verge of a NEGOTIATION.

So what is the difference in technique that differentiates between selling, haggling and negotiating? Let me explain:

Selling

This is not a book about **selling** per se, so you will need to read some books on selling and business persuasion (especially the ones I've written of course – see the list at the end of the book!) for detailed instructions on how to go about selling your things, products, services and ideas to other people. However this brief explanation will help you understand the process and avoid, whenever possible, having to negotiate in the first place.

When you have a product, service or idea to sell, you have to begin long before you meet the potential buyer(s) with a simple question to yourself and it is this: "What problem is my product, service or idea there to solve?" The reason for this essential self question is that *you have no other value to your prospective customers or business partners than your ability to solve at least one problem for them* ... maybe more than one. This is such an important point that I am going to repeat it again: **You have no other value to your prospective customers or business partners than your ability to solve at least one problem for them.**

A lot of well-intentioned sellers (individuals and organizations) just don't *get* this basic concept of commerce, but it is true nevertheless. They have an idea which they think will be a huge business hit. Without bothering to research or test their market they spend a fortune on developing the product or service. They then spend a further fortune on headed paper, business cards, computers, copiers, websites and office space. Then they hit a brick wall: **customers**! Where are they? Why isn't the phone ringing? Where are the Internet enquiries?

The reason is that all human beings are fundamentally in this life for themselves; they are not *against* you ... they just are *for* themselves. In general there is only one unconditional relationship in all our lives: the one between ourselves and our children (or your parents and you). Everything else, every business and personal relationship, has this statement and accompanying caveat hanging over it:

"I love you."

*Terms and conditions apply

As a business owner myself I quite like people to like me and I hope they like my training business but it isn't the final reason people employ us. It IS true that when humans make their initial purchasing decisions or open their minds to the possibility that they might be persuaded, they are making their decision at a deeply subconscious and emotional level. We all like pleasant people who we can relate to, so it will always pay you to aim to be "likeable" (more on this later in the book). But potential customers and business partners always rationalize that decision with facts before finally buying the product service or idea.

A man without a smiling face shouldn't open a shop.

Chinese Proverb

But no prospective customer sits in their office saying to themselves, "I think we'll get our staff trained in some business skills ... just ... just ... well ... 'because!' I'll look on the Internet and see who has the longest list of training programmes. Then who ever has, a) the longest list, b) seems like a nice guy and c) in my opinion also has the biggest need to increase their profits ... that's who I'll choose."

Neither do prospective customers sit in their office, organizing an internal training programme themselves, suddenly stop and say, "Hang on ... we could do this ourselves but why don't we cut old Bob Etherington in? He's a decent fellow ... and I'm sure he could do with the business ... let's give him a call."

A really shocking statistic in my own experience of running a company in the past few years is that on not one single occasion has anyone taken up any references on me or my company prior to employing us. I have offered prospective customers a list of current customer names. They are never contacted. Our own website features one of those "About Us" headings; Internet surfers seeking our type of business, rarely go to that page.

The real reason that our, or any, business exists or that people (you and me) buy products, articles and services is for one reason ... to solve a problem. If customers believe you or I can solve, or might be able to solve, a specific problem because our websites say so, *then* they make contact.

So as a seller, in order to minimize the chance that you may have to negotiate, your first thought must be: What problem is my idea, article, asset, product or service (the one I'm intending to sell) able to solve?

Once you have written that down on a piece of paper (I'm a great believer in "writing-down", it makes your vague concept[s] totally concrete) you can prepare your selling strategy. In general this selling strategy of yours should focus on those identified problem areas. And the way to make people (potential customers) "focus" on the problem-solving benefits of your proposition, is not to "tell" them too much or talk at them. But instead, ask them questions about some of these potential problems your proposition could solve.

The more you ask questions about the usefulness of the potential benefits of your proposition the more the mind of your potential persuade-ee will focus on your proposition.

It is a horrible, but undeniable, truth that most intending "sellers" get themselves into a situation where they eventually have to "negotiate" because they simply say or tell too much during the earlier selling attempt. But all top business persuaders know one thing for sure: "telling isn't selling".

A big pile or list of "facts" fired at your target prospective customer about your proposition, is a grand way to build up a wall of rejection. If that is what you want, because you actually WANT to *negotiate*, please carry on.

But facts don't sell.

Telling doesn't sell.

A "big pile of your stuff" doesn't sell.

On the other hand, chatty, conversational questions about your proposition which allow you to *identify the problems your customer is seeking to solve*, do sell. Once you have identified what the person on the other side of the table is looking for, that's all you talk about; nothing else.

Research shows that 80% of objections during a basic, simple "sale" are caused by the seller saying too much. Very often the sale is already made in the customer's head then the seller adds in some uncalled for facts (under the misguided apprehension that a lot of added stuff will "sugar" the sale and increase the probability of a sale) only to have it blow up in their face. Then they are inevitably on the road to a negotiation.

You think people are too sensible to wreck a sale in this way in the real world? Not a bit of it! A few years ago I was working in New York, as a sales trainer and accompanied a sales executive (responsible for selling a sophisticated, online, financial information product) to a major client. In the course of the discussion with the client the luckless executive led us "up the garden path" straight into a negotiation in what should have been a very (very) simple sale.

The customer in question knew the product he wanted and all we had to do was call in, get a contract signed and walk out. What could be simpler than that? So we met the customer in his office, he signed the contract and we prepared to leave. And then the sales executive said the words that subsequently forced us into that *negotiation*! The seller said, (and only he knows why!) "As we're here and I've brought my laptop why don't I just go through all the things that you will be able to do when you have access online to our product?!" Then, without further ado, he opened his laptop and launched into an impromptu demonstration.

AAARGHHH!

The customer politely stood there looking ever so slightly disinterested – after all he knew what he wanted the product for and therefore why he had just signed the contract for a great deal of money; he *knew* that is, until a critical moment was reached!

The sales executive decided to show a part of the product that allowed the user to display a large amount of numerical information as a chart or graph on the screen. This woke up the customer immediately! "I hate all this graphics and technical analysis!!" he said. "Now I come to think of it, I didn't realize this was part of the product. I really don't need all that stuff ... I don't like it ... all mumbo jumbo. I just want access to the numbers. I tell you what ... take that part out of the product or bar us from accessing it and [*OH NO...here it comes*] give me a discount!"

Catastrophe!

There was no way that it was possible to "customize" this particular online product to meet this customer's need; it was all or nothing. If the salesman had said nothing the customer would have been quite happy with his purchase and would never have accessed the offending graphics package. It would have been there, in the product ... just never looked at.

So there and then the customer asked for the signed contract to be handed back while we "had a think" about how we would deliver *exactly* what he wanted. The upshot was that it then took us several more weeks of "negotiation" to arrive at a mutually acceptable solution. We did end up with the same revenue and we did not alter the product. But the final "deal" involved a great deal more compromise and free addons for normally chargeable services than would have been necessary had we only had the common sense not to showoff unrequested features in the first place!

If you'd prefer a simple "sale" rather than a protracted negotiation, remember this: never make a statement when you could ask a question! Simply put, questions are your primary persuasive tool and a great way to avoid having to *negotiate*.

So what if you're the buyer ... what's in it for you?

If you're the potential buyer in a "potentially simple" sales or persuasive transaction and you also want to avoid a negotiation, make sure you too take the trouble to write down, on a piece of paper, exactly why you want to buy the product, proposition or service. Write down how much it's worth to you. Write down the problems you're seeking to solve if you are to agree a deal. You too should aim to ask as many questions as possible (he or she who asks most questions controls the sale). In most cases you, the buyer, are in the stronger position ... don't give up your power. Most professional sales people have been trained in some powerful selling techniques.

A few years ago I decided to have the very large roof space in my house converted into another bedroom. Knowing what I know and having learnt most of it in the "school of hard knocks", I sat down with a sheet of paper and wrote down everything I needed: a fixed price contract; a five year guarantee; no tight spiral staircase squeezed into a corner but a full size open, straight-staircase that matched the one in the lower part of the house; full height ceilings; built-in wardrobes; no change to the exterior roof shape of the house; running hot and cold water and a sink to wash in; fully insulated; and four large windows to keep it all very bright. I had done my research around many competing companies and I knew what I wanted to pay and what I expected to get for my money.

The salesman from the loft conversion company came with his presentation folder and (as usual) began to completely over-sell all the must-have extras. But I neither wanted nor needed:

electric window blinds, a shower stall, additional windows, full furnishing service ... he did his best but they just weren't on my list because I didn't want a negotiation; I wanted a simple sale.

Letting him complete his classic 30 minute "sales pitch" actually allowed me to haggle the sale price down in about 10 minutes. "Hmmmmm ... (big pause) ... so what if we *don't* have the blinds, the shower, the extra windows and do our own furnishing ... how much then?"

Not (luckily for me) being versed in the skills of negotiation (a true, common or garden *negotiating virgin* in fact), he agreed to a big discount thinking that "price" was my *big* issue. Most sellers do ... poor fools! And within an hour he had agreed to a greatly discounted sale price but he had a sale. And I was pleased because it was what I wanted (especially the fixed price contract) and so at that moment was he.

A few months later however with the inevitable set-backs and unexpected costs that occur in this type of project, the fixed price bit was looking decidedly wobbly for the contractor. Trying to preserve a modicum of his originally anticipated profit, he tried to persuade me to have even fewer windows and a very narrow staircase (he even had such a staircase made ... hoping I wouldn't notice I suppose; he subsequently had to have another full-width one made) and not have the sink either ... "Not really practical mate".

But had the contractor's salesman been trained to sell effectively, the contractor would never have been in this situation in the first place. And if in addition the contracting company had also trained their sales person to "negotiate" they would have (or could have) ended up with a very sensible, wise and efficient deal instead of allowing me to control the outcome.

The sales process, provided you learn how to control it whether you are a buyer or a seller, is by far the quickest method of completing a commercial transaction. If you are unable to complete such a simple sale however you do additionally need to know how to negotiate and so end up with a deal which gives both parties – you and the other side – what they are seeking. I am often asked by the way, "What if everybody in business reads your books, attends your training ourses and starts following the processes you describe? Won't there be constant deadlocks because then we all know what and why the others are behaving as they do and proposing what they propose?"

In theory you might be right. But after three and a half decades in the field I can tell you that most people in business, in every country in the world, read all the books (mine and other people's), watch the training DVDs and attend the training courses … then … carry on as before – no change. Don't ask me why … they just do. But if you follow what I and many other practicing and successful business communicators and sellers tell you, I promise you'll get the commercial outcomes you desire.

Haggling

Many people believe that "haggling" and "negotiating" are interchangeable terms. This is not true. Haggling is what Brian and Harry the Haggler are demonstrating in the *Life of Brian* excerpt in the Introduction of this book. Haggling is what you do when you're buying a six-year-old second-hand car from a stranger after seeing it in a "classified ad" in your local paper.

You: So just remind me how much are you asking for this?
Seller: Three thousand five hundred pounds [Seven thousand US Dollars].
You: That seems a lot for a car this age.
Seller: Well it is only six years old and in very good condition.
You: I was thinking it would be more like fifteen hundred. Would you accept that?

Seller: Fifteen hundred!? ... it's only got 20,000 miles on the clock. Three two-fifty is the best I can do.

You: But look here, there are a few signs of rust just here along the bottom of the door ... I will have to fix those ... it will take me time and goodness knows what else I will find ... It's roughly the type of car I want though ... Tell you what ... I'll give you eighteen hundred ... cash!

Seller: No, I'm sorry I will have no trouble selling this for at least two nine-fifty ... it has really low mileage for a reliable car this age.

You: Two nine-fifty? For a rusty six-year-old car? The best I can do, and this is my final offer is ... [and so on]

Haggling is mostly about price and nothing else. Over and over again I am told by sales people in London, Glasgow, Dublin, Oslo, Houston TX, New York, Toronto, Hong Kong, Singapore, Tehran, Sydney, Baku, Paris and just about any city you could mention, that their product IS too expensive and therefore they must ... MUST ... be prepared to discount it.

OK ... If you only want to learn how to haggle here's how:

If as a *virgin negotiator* you still insist on equating haggling with negotiating and don't want to take a bit of prep-time to organize yourself a little better in order to negotiate *better value* deals, then I can offer you a few tips on pure haggling.

Despite all the foregoing and when you are never likely (or rarely likely) ever to do business with somebody, or a company, again, haggling is a great way for you to save hundreds – often many thousands – of Pounds, Dollars, Euros or indeed any world currency. If you are a "buyer" in a global market place where many poorly trained sellers eventually come to believe that their product is just one of several similar "commoditised" products or services you can usually easily persuade them, by haggling, to cut their prices ... or you'll go elsewhere.

But as we have already discussed most Northern Hemisphere people absolutely hate to haggle. Many people who perceive themselves as "sophisticated" think it makes them look cheap. And yet they're positive that someone else, somewhere, is getting a better price for the same thing.

People equate haggling with arguing. Men especially don't convert thoughts into speech as quickly as women can. This is why they are often at a distinct disadvantage in an argument with a woman. It is also why it is wrongly thought that the "gift of the gab" is key to coming out on top of a business deal. But the only thing you need to haggle the lowest possible price is:

1. Determination; and
2. A pocketful of mystic lines.

LINE 1: "WELLLL ... I'M REALLY NOT SURE ..."

I went shopping for new car tyres recently in one of those nationwide UK tyre fitting places. Because I'm a boy racer at heart and own a car which requires some rather expensive tyres I thought I was probably going to be out of pocket by at least one thousand pounds (USD 2000) for four tyres. In the tyre fitters, just across the road from where I live, I was offered three at £250 each and the fourth free – or £187 per tyre (plus £50 for fitting).

Not bad; but being only two miles away from another similar outlet I drove down to compare and see if they could beat the price. The owner of this franchise said he could do £150 per tyre – £37 less than the other place. I asked him if that included fitting too. He said he could do it for £40 – £10 less than the other's £50.

I said nothing (big silent pause ... [NEVER underestimate the power of silence]) and kept my mouth shut for what to him must have seemed like an eternity. Finally the owner said he would also offer free nationwide tyre insurance, to replace the tyres if they were ever punctured, saving £60 – and giving me a total saving of £210.

Silence is a great motivator because most people hate it. They will do anything to break a silence of only a few seconds. Be brave, hang on ... for 30 seconds or more if you have enough courage. Most people will break the silence inside 15 seconds. Your silence says to the other person that you are "on the fence" and one more little offer will reel you in. The golden rule here is the same unwritten rule that governs domestic spats when frosty silence settles on the "happy home": *the person who speaks first loses!*

LINE 2: "PLEASE HELP ME TO USE MY MONEY IN YOUR SHOP"

I was in Tottenham Court Road in London recently, which as every Londoner knows is the main "electronic goods" street in the capital. I was just another customer looking for a really good deal on a 37-inch Japanese flat-screen television.

To improve my chance of getting a good deal, I stopped at one of the large shops on a drizzly, late-September Monday at 10am. It was a time I knew the mass of potential customers would be back at work from their summer vacations and business would inevitably be slow. The salesman showed me three TVs – for £1600, £1400 and £999. I told him I only had £700 to spend.

The salesperson told me I could have the lowest price television for £900. I told him the best price I could rise to was £725. "That just isn't possible," the salesman said. He was laughing. Now, these shops in Tottenham Court Road are usually family owned rather than national chains and there are always plenty of salespeople leaning on the counters chatting. So I always reckon there must be a significant profit margin locked into each sale to cover all their salary costs. And at this point in the proceedings a patriarchal figure came and stood next to us; I guessed he was the owner: "Can I help?" "Look," I said. "Please help me spend my money with you. If I don't, my wife is up at Heals [a very large up-market furniture store on the same road] and she is out to buy furniture."

The patriarch proposed £850 if I paid by cash. I said I had to call my wife in Heals. This established that the two of us were going to do the deal. I stepped into the shop doorway and apparently made a mobile phone call. Half a minute later I went back into the shop. "It's good news, she said I can spend £760. So we have a deal?" The owner finally gave in.

Prices on the vast majority of expensive items are "haggleable". Maybe not in chain stores or Harrods or Saks Fifth Avenue but in most other places. You just have to find the right person (preferably the owner) who can do the deal and has an emotional attachment to the bottom line, and then have the courage to ask.

LINE 3: "YOUR COMPETITORS WILL DO IT FOR LESS"

I am often faced by this classic "sales objection" when selling my own services and I am pretty well able to listen and re-sell the perception of value in order to avoid having to "discount". The good news is that (as I have said before in this book) most people who sell, believe that they ARE too expensive and that cost is the main decider. So when you are looking for a low cost deal you can generally haggle them lower by introducing the competitive element. When I wanted to book several rooms in a hotel in Geneva for a training course I went to *booking.com* to find out which hotels recent visitors rated best for all round service. I asked the three highest rated to give me a quote for 20 rooms, over five nights and a conference suite.

I called the two with the lowest prices – the most expensive one (with great views over Lake Geneva) probably wasn't going to discount enough to be competitive – I told the other two that the choice was between them. Then I asked if they could reduce the price.

Both of them telephoned me the next day. Naturally I went with the lowest price and made a saving of over £2800 on the week and still had an almost-as-good view of Lake Geneva. I always say to companies, "Yes you're entitled to make a profit, but if your competitors can do it for less, your company probably can as well".

LINE 4: "I FEEL AS IF I'VE BEEN TRICKED"

One Friday morning recently I went into a local branch of a well-known London hardware store chain. I was buying some electric light bulbs and other domestic bits and pieces for the office. As I was checking-out I saw that there was a special offer of a 50% discount on very handy looking electric car polisher: "Normally £30 ... Special Offer £15!" "Not bad," I thought. "I'll have one," and put it in my basket. It was only when I got back to the office and looked at my receipt I noticed that I had been charged the full £30 for the polisher.

The telephone number was on the receipt so I called the shop. The manager said there was nothing she could do about it because the shop ads all said (OK in small print), that the offer was only available on the Bank Holiday Monday after that weekend. I said that "caveat emptor" ("Let the buyer beware") notwithstanding I felt tricked and that from my point of view, as a customer, the store was baiting consumers, promising a discount in "big writing" that wasn't available for another three days. The manager considered my point and by way of compensation offered me a voucher for £20. I accepted it.

The rule here is don't get angry. You will get yourself into what top hagglers and negotiators call a "Defend and Attack" spiral. Talk first about how you *feel* as a customer. You stand a much greater chance of getting what you want if you are an innocent unhappy victim rather than an unnecessarily angry shopper.

LINE 5: "YOUR BUSINESS BROKE THE PROMISE"

Here's one that worked the other way round and I ended up having to compensate one of my haggling customers. In my business we *occasionally* advertise open-seminars in the UK press. The advertisement instructs potential attendees to: "Call now us now on 0207 486 4008 and book your seat today". But on this particular day the whole telephone system had gone wrong at a human level, and keen customers were telephoning us, not getting to speak to anyone, leaving voice mails and not being called back.

One lady customer finally tracked me down to my mobile phone late in the evening. She was both frustrated and extremely annoyed. "Your advertising is wholly misleading!" she said. "I have called your company three times today and each time somebody promised to call me back inside 30 minutes and nothing has happened. I am very surprised that a company that teaches sales and customer retention is so lax when it comes returning calls. How do you stay in business?!"

She was right. The simplest way to satisfy her apart from a profuse apology was to offer her the five tickets she wanted completely free of charge. She accepted them ... cash advantage to her: a saving of nearly £500.

However a few months later when we once again advertised a repeat presentation of the same seminar she bought and paid for fifteen tickets. Which only goes to prove the old customer service rule: A customer who has had a problem with your company that you have admitted and fixed to their satisfaction, is more loyal than a customer who has never had a problem.

So whenever a company or shop breaks its promise, you have every right to expect something in return. Just make sure you know, beforehand what you want when you're asked.

Negotiating

Negotiating, on the other hand, is about creating value for yourself and your counterparty. Sometimes in a negotiation you end up paying the same as before but getting more value from the deal. Sometimes, when you negotiate, you get less money but the overall value is greater.

A prime and very simple example of such a negotiated outcome for my business can be easily illustrated in the example of a recent enquiry we had from the owner of a magazine publishing company in the UK. He urgently wanted some phone-sales training for his sales staff. We iscussed his requirements and the problems he needed any training to address.

I asked him a lot of focused questions and, as a result, he told me about his current issues and the probable knock-on effects of his not fixing the current malaise in his business. I even managed to get him to tell me how much his business was losing every month and what would happen if his advertising sales didn't improve soon. In fact I did everything that a well-trained sales person should do. By the end of two or three more meetings he was clearly keen to fix the problem and for me to reveal the best solution.

When I presented the recommended programme which would fix his specific problem he was really keen to proceed. When the price was placed on the table however, he sat back in his chair and sighed. "That's expensive!" he said. "But I was expecting it would be in that range ... however I've been checking you out and you were recommended. And yet the current state of our P&L account is not that great. But *if* you insist, I'll pay the fee because we DO need this urgently. On the other hand I'd like to suggest another way to proceed. You see, we print and publish the in-flight magazines for a number of international airlines. We are prepared, in exchange for your company delivering this training programme for us, to offer you, free of charge, three months, single-page advertising space (right hand page, in colour – the most valuable position), in the following magazines." He then listed many of the magazines you'll find in the seat pockets of some of the world's leading airlines.

It didn't take a moment to work out how many tens of thousands of captive-audience, international business people, would see such an ad. I also calculated very rapidly how much I would normally have to pay to reach so many prospective customers: several tens of thousands of pounds. For me the value he was offering was far more than we would earn from running a single training programme for his company.

Yet for him and his publishing house, it was an easy giveaway. From his point of view he was offering me a single blank white page which had little intrinsic value. It was simply an approximately A4 sized piece of paper that could be added in or omitted from a magazine without anyone noticing. But the value he was exchanging this page for, in the case of his company, was equally large ... a top quality telephone training programme for almost no direct cost. We very rapidly agreed the deal and both walked away smiling. Very little money would change hands (just travel and accommodation expenses in fact) but the value to both parties was enormous.

It was a very simple negotiation but one which produced the most important outcomes I can think of when it comes to modern business transactions: Nobody felt they had been dealt a worse hand than anyone else, everybody felt the other person had understood their position, everybody would be willing to do business with the other party again.

I have since negotiated other similar simple deals with other businesses in areas in which we can more or less barter our services. They have all resulted in the parties coming away with greater mutual value than had we concentrated solely on the direct cash. These include website hosting, stationery supplies and even limousine hire. Despite what you may think it is rarely just "the money".

SECTION 4

Deconstructing the "No"

Having now analysed the differences between pure *selling*, price *haggling* and *negotiating* it is time to consider how we should plan and prepare for any real *value based negotiation*.

Before you can begin to consider whether a negotiation (or even buying this book) is worth your time or effort there are a couple of things we need to agree.

- Other people do things for their own reasons ... not your reasons. You will rarely persuade another person to do anything ... people persuade themselves.
- Nobody will negotiate with you unless they think you can offer them a benefit or cause them some difficulty.

The situation that necessitates a "Negotiation" in the first place is often that two parties have already taken up (or would otherwise take up) apparently intransigent and irreconcilable positions:

"I want what I want and that's it ... and 'No', I'm not moving!"

"Well I want what I want too and 'No' I'm not moving either!"

One very simple example, which can be used to illustrate this dilemma is to consider "The Twelve Oranges"!

To do this, imagine that you are a fitness fanatic who has arisen early in the morning and walked down to the local corner-shop and purchased twelve oranges. These you bring home and place in the refrigerator with the aim of coming home from work later that day, getting changed, going for a one hour run then coming home again and squeezing the cool oranges before enjoying a refreshing orange drink.

However when you DO arrive home to enjoy your eagerly awaited orange drink, you find that your partner has removed your oranges from the refrigerator and has them on the kitchen table. He (or she) is clearly in the middle of making a cake ... an orange cake!

"What are you doing ... with my oranges?" you cry.

"I am making a cake for our friend's birthday tomorrow," your partner replies. "They're just oranges ... don't make such a fuss you can buy some more."

"But the shop is shut now!" you say. "I wanted them tonight ... they are my oranges. I want the oranges. No, I *need* the oranges!"

"Well I want the oranges," says your partner. "I have told our friend I will bring this cake and I will. I *need* the oranges!"

So *"virgin negotiator"* here's the first lesson in the quest for negotiation preparation. When two parties are staring at each other in such a mock-standoff situation how can it be resolved? What can you possibly suggest as ways of deconstructing the "NOs" which will give satisfaction to both parties?

The first thing to do is consider all the possible solutions:

- You could for example divide the oranges in half: you get six; your partner gets six. *In this ompromise situation both parties feel as if they have lost something.*
- You could persuade your partner to give up the oranges today and make a cake with another flavour. *In this case you feel as if you won but your partner feels as if they lost.*
- You could be persuaded to give up the oranges today. *If this happens you are likely to feel slightly aggrieved that you lost whilst your partner feels as if the win has been for them.*

These and other cutting, dividing, giving and taking solutions are not particularly satisfactory. They certainly don't allow much possibility for a win-win solution. So what's to be done? The answer is usually very simple and was actually contained in a book I bought a few years ago whilst living in New York. It was a book on how to get absolutely anything you want. On the first page it gave the simple advice: "Ask for it!"

Questions and information are the primary tools of both top sellers and top negotiators.

Questions allow you to start understanding the other side's interests.

Questions invite the other side to speak while you shut up. This alone is a surprisingly powerful and persuasive gift which you appear to be offering any other party in a negotiation.

The reason for this powerful perception is that:

- Human beings place more value on the words that come out of their own mouths than anything they hear.
- Human beings place more value on the things they request rather than un-requested things they are freely offered.

So when you ask somebody for their thoughts, opinions or feelings you gain a number of useful benefits. Most of all you start to get behind the reason for their "No". And if you employ it on yourself or your side's "No" you start to understand yours too.

Employing this questioning tool to deconstruct the "No" in the case of "The Twelve Oranges" it would pay you to stop and ask yourself questions like: What is an orange composed of? Is it one thing or a combination of elements that make the fruit? Does the cook need all the elements? Do I need all the elements?

This process may lead to a direct question to the cook: "Can you tell me how you will use the oranges in your cake ... do you need the whole of each orange?" Inevitably you would discover that the cook had little interest in the juice but requires the one thing you have no use for: the orange peel. As a result you discover that you can both have exactly what you want from the oranges ... you the juice, your partner the peel.

By asking the right questions you have "Deconstructed the No" and actually reached the Valhalla of all top negotiators ... a win-win!

Good negotiated agreements "Deconstruct the No", by focusing on all the parties' interests, rather than their "positions".

A so-called "position" is a (apparently) fixed place which you are currently occupying and from which you cannot or will not budge. You can imagine it as a square on the chessboard ... a rung of the ladder ... a place in the race ... a price you want for something you are selling ... a price beyond which you will not pay more as a buyer.

Behind each position are your "interests". Your interests are the things that have caused and are still causing you to maintain that position. In other words the moves on the chessboard that have brought you this far and the current positions of other chess pieces around you that are keeping you there ... the steps you have taken up the ladder to this place and the fact that there are no further rungs to enable you to climb higher ... the number of people you have overtaken in the race and your opinion about your ability to overtake those still in front ... the costs invested in producing your product which dictate the minimum profit margin you must secure and the fact that all your other customers always pay that price ... your need to obtain the product you desire but not at the price currently on offer and your willingness to offer some other service to the seller which may fill the price gap.

The disadvantage of defining the problem which has brought you to the negotiating table in terms of your individual "positions" means that at least one side involved in the negotiation will "lose" in the deal.

But when the problem is defined in terms of both parties' underlying "interests", it is often possible to "Deconstruct the No" in such a way that both parties' interests are satisfied.

The art of man-management is to get people to agree to do voluntarily those things that must be done anyway.

Kenneth H. Blanchard, The One Minute Manager

So if you are in a negotiation which, for example, is getting into a conflict over who is to do what by when on some project, endeavour not to argue about who is right and who is wrong.

You are *not* there to prove you are right! (*This is a "position".*) You are there to come to an agreement and get things moving.

Instead, ask questions before and after the negotiation which will reveal the interests behind the positions. Then look at the possible reasons why the various people feel the way they do.

Why does one person at the table feel that his deadline is unfair and another believe that hers is impossible to meet? Is there something that you can do to make his workload more manageable without placing an unfair workload on the other people on the team? Is the one worried about her deadline actually telling you she doesn't feel sufficiently confident in an area that a bit of one-on-one coaching would fix. Always try to discover what the needs and interests are underneath a person's demands or "positions" in order to find out what the real problem is about. Very often, it is a problem that can be solved to your mutual advantage if it is handled openly.

Always be thinking, "Why did he just say that?" "What made her react in that way?" "Why is she saying she must have her own office?" "What is the real concern they have about our price ... what are they comparing us with?"

Another example of my own need to "Deconstruct a No" happened to me just last summer ... this time in my private life, because I like to go flying. I don't own a plane so I regularly hire one from a local flying club. What happened was that on a bright summer's morning, in early July, due to an administrative mix-up, the plane I had booked, had also been double booked to another club member on the same day. We both arrived at the same time and realized what had happened. (The mental *unspoken* arguments were clearly building.)

"I booked it first ... look!"

"Well I'm afraid I've booked it too." (Yes like all humans we were taking up positions.)

"Well I really must have it you know ... I have two other people as passengers here who were looking forward to a day out with me."

"Well Bob I have to fly this weekend because my licence will expire unless I maintain my minimum hours."

We couldn't both have it ... so how did we deconstruct our "Nos"? The first task was to ascertain – and share – the reason(s) I wanted the aircraft and the reason(s) he wanted it.

Me: To go to France for the day; because I needed the practice to keep my licence hours up; because I enjoy flying; because I had two friends (passengers) with me who would otherwise be greatly disappointed.

Him: Because he needed the licence practice hours too; because he enjoys flying; because he was going up for three hours only; because he liked that particular aircraft; there were no other aircraft available.

Once we appreciated our individual "interests" behind what would have been a brick wall of "Nos", we were able to line up enough common interests to come to an agreement.

Result? I invited him to join us for a day out in France. He agreed ... I flew us there; he flew us back in the evening. He did the radio and the navigation going out ... I did it coming back. We all had a great day out and we both got our practice flying.

Had all the seats in the aircraft been occupied in my case, making such a share impossible, we would probably have found other interests ... our flying club management's for example ... what is their likely key interest? To keep two members happy. They might therefore have subcontracted a plane from another club at the airfield. Or maybe offered a discounted hire on another day for the party that surrendered their day out.

Once you start to "deconstruct the No's" it is rare not to discover some parallel common interests which allows any ... well "most" impasses to be broken.

So, does "Deconstructing the No" by identifying interests rather than positions always bring about a successful resolution in negotiations? Alas not in my experience. After all if it did there might be no more wars and combative countries would have first sat down at a table and discussed their interests and then again World War II might never had happened ... oh and everything in the garden would be lovely! Yeah right!

A few years ago I was involved with a company accused by a rival of stealing some corporate information. The accusation was strongly denied as nasty corporate smear. The matter was eventually settled out of court as there was insufficient evidence to be sure of either side winning the case. However by then the damage had been done. There was no trust left between them but there was a huge pile of seething animosity.

Eighteen months later the two companies were asked by a mutual and very large international customer to work together to provide a particular seamless service to the large customer. To do this we two "enemies" had to "negotiate" a partnership deal. It was going to be against all human nature to expect either side to consider the interests of the other side. Just asking the question, "Can you tell us why you loathe us?" would have been like pouring gasoline on the fire.

Sybil Fawlty: Can I do anything to help, Basil?

Basil Fawlty: Yes ... go away and kill yourself!

Fawlty Towers

In this case what we did was quite the opposite of, "Deconstructing our respective Nos". We actually focused on our positions and so did they. We decided on the package deal we could live with and so did they. As with so many similar negotiations when real animosity rules we didn't follow the classic: point by point agreement ... move on ... summarize ... new point ... agreement ... move on. As with the sort of "negotiations" that accompany many marital splits we came up with a whole package of what we wanted or rather what we thought we could get away with. This type of "exception that proves the rule" negotiating strategy enables you to indicate the give and take trade-offs you might make. And also, when they see your package, it allows you to gauge their reaction and see what parts of their package might be tradeable in exchange.

You are never going to be trusting partners again ... you are probably never willingly going to seek to work with each other again. The negotiation simply provides a forum for dividing up the spoils and for both sides getting the most for themselves. The only mutual interest is a realization that if they don't settle something then lawyers will take an increasingly large share of the available assets in payment.

SECTION 5

Dealing with "Johnny Foreigner"

> "I do not like thee, Doctor Fell,
> The reason why I cannot tell;
> But this I know, and know full well,
> I do not like thee, Doctor Fell."
>
> TOM BROWN
> A STUDENT AT OXFORD UNIVERSITY IN 1680
> WRITING ABOUT THE THEN DEAN, DR JOHN FELL

There are plenty of weighty academic tomes out there covering the "science" of negotiating. Yet when "virgin negotiators" endeavour to apply the science they often discover that the actions of the person or people on the other side of their negotiation don't allow them to exercise "the theory". This is because those "other people" are unpredictable, emotional, "human beings".

I was leading a "brush-up" workshop recently for some senior international negotiators in a very large company and it was clear that one of them (appointed "Leader" for the day) had a very simple negotiating strategy; he just said "No". It didn't matter what the other team members on his side, in the various negotiating "role-play" business scenarios, suggested, he always said it wouldn't work. In the sessions in which they met counterparties across the negotiating table he said, "No" to almost all their proposals. When they broke off for the occasional "time-out" team discussions, he always suggested that the reaction to new proposals should be "No". His regular mantra was, "Of course it wouldn't happen like this in real life!" In the end his own team, who had some very good ideas which would have broken the barriers in the negotiations, sat back and stopped contributing. Some of the more junior members were completely intimidated and just stared at the table top or out of the window.

During the lunch break on the first day, some of the other members of the team came to me to complain about their colleague. "He won't shut up." "He talks all the time." "He never listens." "I had an idea but I couldn't get a word in edgeways." "He's so negative." "The other side are getting fed up with him too ... I can see that clearly!"

During the coffee break, a couple of hours later, I decided to discuss with him his negotiating and overall personal style. He was an older man (OK he was about my age!) and in a company in which youth is clearly and increasingly "at the helm", reluctantly approaching the twilight of his career. He was probably wondering why he – with all his experience and age – had been placed in what could be seen as a "remedial" class and was out to show no sign of slow down or weakness. One lady on his five-person team (women are five times more perceptive than men) had already told me that his eyes looked "frightened". So I decided not to admonish him in any way but to "chat-him-up" a bit. (Remembering, as Queen Victoria's Prime Minister, Disraeli said, "Everyone loves flattery. But with Royalty you lay it on with a trowel.")

"You're clearly a very experienced negotiator," I said. "Do you still do much in the field?" "Oh yes," he said. "But I'm not really a 'leader' like I am in this workshop. In my real job I lead and 'strategise' but from the back-room in an influencing/advisory role."

"That's great," said I. "How do you think we can bring out some of the other younger people here? They haven't got your experience and I'd like to see how they perform; how could we do that?"

Once again, (in true negotiator style you'll notice) I was trying to focus on his *interests* (a clear need to feel needed and respected) not his *positions* (greying, grumpy, old man!). But he brightened up immediately.

"I think I should do the same in this workshop," he said. "If it's OK with you I'm going to 'lead' in an advisory role after the break, but appoint one of the others as 'the leader'."

"How can we find out how much they're all learning?" I ventured.

"I'll ask them about their strategic approach during the sessions for the rest of this week," he said. "I'll make them think a bit when they get it wrong. That's the best way for them to learn."

That was the turning point for him in the rest of the programme. My "Abominable No-man" (I eventually told him what I'd nicknamed him) discovered the instant change that occurs in other people's perception of you when you shut up and start to ask *them* to articulate *their* ideas, thoughts and opinions.

Not only that, but when you start to listen and understand the way the people, on the other side of the table are thinking you get a much better idea of their interests. And when you do that, your own "No" position often looks really ridiculous even to you (and even if nobody actually says, "I told you so").

In essence other people, just like you and me, simply want to feel good about themselves. And they feel particularly good about themselves if they feel that you respect both them and their culture and that you are listening to them – not just trying to prove that you are right!

People are generally not against you ... they are simply FOR themselves. And apart from being apparently locked in an impenetrable negative mindset like the man in the example above, people present us with loads of other problems too: people don't understand us; people get emotional; people look different from us; people act differently; people talk differently; people are too aggressive; people are too passive; people have different priorities; people don't listen. And so on and so on.

So if "people" are some of the main problem areas we face in a negotiation what can we do about it and why should we do anything about it?

As we have already seen, a good working relationship helps us to deal with our differences and opens up the communication and hence the negotiation. A poor one can sink a deal or a team even when, theoretically, had they got their relationship sorted out in the first place, an agreed deal would have benefited everyone.

I have negotiated deals with people I, sometimes quite irrationally, haven't liked and who have (occasionally!?) not liked me. I have also negotiated with people whose values are quite different from mine and vice versa. Business and commercial activities are not a popularity parade. Not "liking" someone is not an excuse for not dealing with them. If this does happen to be the way you judge a negotiation's usefulness to you, then you will leave a great many business doors flapping open for people like me to walk in and pinch your business.

Like all relationships, marriage included, you have to work at them to make them work ... they usually don't just happen.

Culture

As we saw in the "perception of reality" illusion, in the first chapter of this book, we all see the world through a different pair of "rose coloured" spectacles. As virgin negotiators it is very easy to mess up a negotiation through our failure to understand this very important fact. For example, here are just a few generalizations which you may find useful to bear in mind before getting involved in a negotiation:

- Most Americans will have no trouble sitting down across a table and starting a negotiation with you within a few minutes of your first meeting. An American doesn't need to know you in order to deal with you; very unlike the Middle East or Asia! Oh yes and an American will usually only give you a business card if he or she is genuinely interested in actually doing business with you. In most Asian countries it means no such thing and is simply a polite gesture ... but make sure in China, Japan, Korea, Malaysia and the Philippines that you hand your business card with BOTH hands. Producing it from your top pocket with one hand is seen as a direct snub.

- If an English person tells you that your proposal is "quite good" he or she is indicating that it is only "fair" at best. Whereas if an American tells you that something is "quite good" the meaning they intend to convey is that it is absolutely excellent!

- Frame your discussions with a Norwegian team in the same materialistic/aspirational terms that you might use to an American or British negotiator and you are likely to find a distinct coldness emanating from them. In Norway such things are important but not mentioned. It is a very egalitarian society underpinned by something they call "Jante Loven" (Jante's Law) which dictates that you should never believe that you are better

than anyone else, you should never "have" more than
another person and you should never "think big".

- In Scandinavian countries in general, if you are invited
  out for a meal and somebody raises a glass of wine
  to toast some person or aspect of the proceedings
  be very careful to meet everyone's eye before
  taking a sip. Simply saying "cheers" and downing
  a gulp is considered the height of rudeness.

- Negotiate in the Middle East and you will find it impossible
  to get any negotiations underway until the other side has
  got to know you as a human being. This may take several
  meetings at which no business is discussed but during
  which (alcohol-free) discussions of a general nature take
  place. It is important for people in this part of the world and
  further east, that they have the full measure of you before
  doing a deal. The actual piece of paper you all sign is more
  symbolic too. Whereas in USA and Europe the contract is
  "all", in many countries and culture the handshake is more
  binding and "honour" and "face" are the driving forces.

- In negotiations with Russians and Iranians hold out firmly
  for your interests in the face of pleading, emotions, anger
  and even tears, to a level which you may never have
  experienced before. They are very proud tough people
  in these countries and expect you to be the same. Make
  your case firmly and listen to theirs at length. If you
  start to compromise too early they WILL regard it as
  a sign of weakness. Some of my most recent training
  deals have been with companies in Tehran and every
  time the ritual has been tough and uncompromising.
  What eventually happens, provided you have taken the
  time to listen to them first (be prepared for a lot of hard
  luck stories and much arcane old-fashioned sounding
  language), is that they suddenly crack and return
  with new proposals which, surprisingly, address your

interests perfectly. Believe me, if they keep returning to the table you have got something they want.

- Oh and table manners. I was always taught, as an English child (as are American, French and Irish children in their respective countries I believe), to keep my elbows off the table, during a meal. I was quite surprised just recently to discover that in Germany a person's hands are always to be kept in sight above the table so "elbows on the table", far from being rude and ill-mannered in Germany, is the done thing in business and polite society.

So does all this really matter?

I'm afraid so; and it can matter a great deal that you recognize that these differences exist between companies and even families in the same country or city. And it matters a lot that you *do* something about it fast if you want a negotiation to succeed. Other people and cultures are not necessarily "wrong". But your thinking that they may be and doing nothing about it, may scupper your chances of moving from virgin negotiator to top-negotiator in their eyes.

Quite recently I was struggling to establish rapport with another English team who we were negotiating with in London (my home town). They worked for a major national oil company from a country that I considered to favour being very formal and well-dressed. So, accordingly, I turned up in a freshly pressed suit, white shirt, nice tie, and mirror-polish shoes. Things started awkwardly however, and I didn't know why. The first meeting laboured on for three hours and I really thought it was not going to turn out in my favour. Nevertheless, towards the end, I suggested that we summarize the discussion so far and stepped up to the flip-chart easel to write up the "bullets". As I did so I took off my jacket and removed my tie. The atmosphere suddenly lightened.

"Thank God for that," said their lead negotiator. "We thought you were really up-tight ... Now let's start having a serious discussion!" The big "cultural" barrier that had been sitting there like the proverbial "elephant in the room" was my tie! These oilmen wore no ties; they were all in open-neck shirts. My tie was a cultural faux pas. The negotiation then continued into the afternoon and the following week the deal was sown up.

Is rapport the answer to everything?

If you take two people from opposite sides of the world and put them together you might think that because we appear to have the same tastes that rapport would be instant. I'm afraid this is not the case. Just because I buy my suits from the same Hong Kong tailor that my prospective Japanese business partner does (*there is an excellent one by the way which visits key world cities and will make you a Saville Row suit at one-third of the London price*) is only the start. That we have both been enjoying the latest Rugby World Cup games on TV, both like the duet from *The Pearl Fishers* and enjoy sampling wines from the Napa Valley in California would make everything fine. Alas no ... our concepts of "correct behaviour" are very different and can easily upset a negotiation.

I recently (well ... about 20 years ago in the example I'm thinking of) spoke for weeks with Ichi San, a potential business partner in Japan, and yet the barriers between us were never broken down – and the deal I wanted was never consummated. On reflection, the problem had to do with our different views of the negotiation process itself and our misinterpretations of each other's behaviour.

For me (trained over the years by many top American and British companies), negotiation was about pushing through a deal; full stop! When I didn't think our discussion was moving forward as quickly as I thought it should, I recall that my arguments became increasingly forceful. Ichi San and I did talk about it years later when we were both employed in New York and met accidentally at the Hilton Hotel. For his part, he told me, he had seen my haste as disrespect so our negotiation essentially ended days before our talks did.

So while globalization, the Internet and rapid communications and marketing have made the world very much smaller in many ways, there are still deep differences between our cultures. Despite similar tastes, Ichi San and I each approached our negotiation in a way very much conditioned by our national cultures. Because we sat down to negotiate without understanding each other's assumptions about the process, all we ended up with was a big fat nothing!

Serious negotiation is nearly always a touchy business, which virgin negotiators must prepare for, because the rewards for you getting it right can be enormous. As the need for a "negotiation" in the first place is often the result of the failure of a previous attempt at a simple "sale and purchase", it requires, in addition to Aspiration (see Chapter 1), further applications of patience and diplomacy in equal measure. But balancing a cross-cultural negotiation, whether that is inter-family, company, city or country, can present a bit of a challenge. So here I have set out some tips that will help you put together a deal with "Johnny Foreigner".

1. PREPARE TO UNDERSTAND

As a trained professional "seller" I can tell you that "prior understanding" of your counterparty's expectations before you attempt to sell anyone anything (ideas, concepts, products or services) is key to getting it right. Your negotiating counterparty's expectations of the negotiation's outcome may well be very different from yours.

Like you, the person across the other side of the table will want to succeed. But success may not mean the same thing to him and his team as it does to you. I nearly wrecked a Norwegian negotiation a few years ago by placing far too much emphasis on a successful "financial" outcome for both sides whilst my counterparties saw success in terms of community cohesion and "more time with their respective families". I only retrieved the situation when one of the "other side" whispered to me in the bar that night that my antics that day had clearly shown them that I "wasn't very Norwegian".

The decision-making process is frequently different too. In America and Europe senior managers usually make decisions alone. In Japan the equivalent managers make decisions by consensus which generally increases the time you need to allow for the negotiation process.

In the West we place a high value on incorporating future flexibility in many deals (because who knows what will happen tomorrow?). However, according to my one time failed negotiating partner, Ichi San, once a Japanese executive has reached a decision and discussed it with his team, he believes it is a shameful "loss of face" to change it.

Your earnest endeavours, before you embark on a negotiation, to understand such underlying attitudes, will help you see the world as your counterparty does and ascertain what your potential partner's priorities are. Then you can adapt your strategy accordingly.

2. BUILD BRIDGES EARLY, TO LEVEL PLAYING FIELDS

All human beings share some similar human experiences with each other. For example, you could select from ... a family ... a place to live in ... a life outside work ... kids ... and so on. So do your best, early on, to find out what you might be able to share with a potential business partner. *Anything* that will allow your "Johnny Foreigner" counterparty to share something with you. With one Japanese businessman I could only discover that he had lived, during an "ex-pat" assignment in England, just outside London in a road adjacent to my own and his children had attended the same school as mine. "Ah Oakwood Avenue ... in Beckenham ... you know it! A very high class road! Very good houses. Many Japanese live locally." Such a very simple link can help you get over "people" issues like pride, excitability, skin colour, personal ego, war footings, "face-saving" and all that complicating "stuff". And it is a very good tactic to establish this link early because these problems can crop up at any time and where you least expect them.

Only once this is done can you seriously begin to consider how you will conduct the negotiation. And to keep it simple, as a negotiating virgin, you have a choice of doing it two ways: "Confrontational" or "Problem-solving."

As a *confrontational negotiator*, you will be a tough and demanding person who makes very few compromises. And this approach, as outlined earlier in this chapter, can be very successful when you are up against one of the cultures that is obviously going to act tough. In this case you either win or lose. But the outcome is rarely or never going to be a conditional agreement.

As a *problem-solving negotiator*, on the other hand, you will need to take a wider view and attempt to get as much as you can without laying down any deal breaking ultimatums. You will establish common ground wherever you can find it and approach the negotiation on a point-by-point basis.

Whilst a virgin negotiator has to be careful about adopting a generalized approach which will apply across all cultures, most of the academic research into the best way to persuade other humans, seems to agree that an understanding, problem-solving approach to cross-cultural negotiations, is the one most likely to result in a successful outcome. This problem-solving approach is the best one to adopt if you want to avoid costly mistakes. Nevertheless it has definite limitations.

For many societies, and this applies particularly to Asian and Middle Eastern cultures, negotiation is a *ritual* especially in the early phases. And you are well advised to find out about these negotiating rituals for any culture you will be sitting across the table from, even if your foreign counterparty turns out not to need them. I have made more negotiating mistakes in this area than anything else! So many in fact that I should write out 100 times: *Not everyone thinks like English people ... Not everyone thinks like English people ... Not everyone thinks...*

So now, for my part, I always endeavour to find, and talk to, someone from the business culture I will be negotiating in. Then I ask them to outline the expected business behaviour in their society and culture ... and I take notes! And the people who can help me often turn out to be located in the local embassy or consulate. If I can't find them there then I Google "culture" and always discover lots and lots of useful information.

Rituals in negotiation are not confined exclusively to "Oriental" negotiations. For example, take one particular country here in Europe: Germany.

In Germany you will often find that you have to spend a large part of the early negotiations in detailed analysis of "the numbers". All the details and numbers usually have to be agreed on first. And some luckless "plod" is generally to be seen head down in their laptop with spreadsheet alive with figures. Their job is to ensure there are no up-front mistakes!! After several years I have discovered that this formal Germanic behaviour is not actually about numeric analysis and perfection. It is simply a ritualized confidence-building procedure in which the two potential counterparties go through a series of routine checks just to display mutual trust.

This is also a society in which addressing someone by his or her first name can be a definite "no-no" in a business setting even after several years of getting to know them. (For the Frankfurt office of Reuters – a company I was employed by for two decades – I was always "Herr Ezzerington" for the full period of my employment.) So in Germany, or in a similar culture, the rapid problem-solving approach, which would try to find common ground quickly, might prove very threatening for those ritual negotiators. They are not "wrong"; it is simply a different way of behaving which you must expect and understand.

When you are up against cultural differences in a negotiation, you need to be aware of the possible adverse effects when a flexible free-style (e.g. American British, Australian) is attempted, in a culture in which a more ritualized formal style (e.g. German, Japanese, Persian) is the normally accepted way. If your "flexibile free-style" is not understood by the other side, they will probably see it as smooth and slippery "alien" behaviour and resent it. This is because they are not trained, or even culturally equipped, from the cradle, to counter it with any similar flexibility. Subsequently you will often see embarrassment on their faces. They will probably be feeling awkward and clumsy ... even inferior. It will subsequently become very difficult for them to believe in your sincerity. They may see your apparent "tactics" as an effort on your part, to lure them on to foreign territory defined by another established group (yours) which will put them at a disadvantage.

If you want people to work with you remember what has been said earlier in this book: help them to feel good about themselves. People are generally not against you ... they are simply FOR themselves.

3. KEEP THINGS UNDER CONTROL

OK, so you have opened up the ideal "problem solving" negotiation. You have built your bridge to the level or "common" playing field. You know something about the other side and have some human life experience that you can share and they know something about you too. Now youhave to think about the next part of your tactical game. Now you can begin to discuss the issues with them and use what you have learnt from your cultural mentor (embassy advisor/consulate person/acquaintance/ Internet) and as far as you can, adjust your behaviour to suit your potential counterparty's culture.

One effective tactic for Italians (and other fast negotiators).

Having spent some considerable time negotiating in Milan I have found that Italians (often talking at great speed and in a comparatively excitable manner compared with many other country's nationals) will often try to batter through this stage at quite a pace. They will repeatedly insist on their terms to wear down their counterparties. Knowing this I have found one very effective tactic in the face of any "Hurry! Hurry! ... Haste! Haste!" ploy is to appear to "lose focus." This is what I do: Imagine a typical situation. Possibly the second or third meeting in the process of a complex negotiation. They clearly want to do business with me or they wouldn't still be sitting there. We have resolved *most* of the issues and the people opposite me want me to make a decision NOW ... before lunch! ... (so they can get their planes home rather than work a bit longer to create a wiser long term outcome). The "other side" are all looking at me (they would like to "railroad" me ... I can see it in their faces). "So what's it to be Bob ... "Yes" ... or ...?"

I look at the table top ... I say nothing ... I slowly ... (very slowly) ... reach into my pocket and take out one of my own company-logo plastic pens. Then (with a great palaver) I have trouble getting the writing end to stay extended when I press the button ... I try several times ... click ... click ... click ... someone offers me an alternative ... I politely decline and slowly twist the top until the spring suddenly pings the top off. I try to reassemble it but it doesn't go together. I try again and it sort-of works ... until I apply it to my writing pad when ... click! ... it all springs apart again. I then slowly reach into my pocket and find another pen ... click ... it works ... now I look up at the rest of the negotiators (slightly dazed) and say, "Oh I'm so sorry! ... I've quite forgotten where we'd got to ... can somebody remind me?"

At the other end of the scale are Chinese negotiators. To succeed in the 21st century take the ability to negotiate with the Chinese very seriously.

In my experience they are terrific negotiators. You will find that they often make one proposal after another in the early stages in order to test the limits of a possible deal you may give them. Get used to silences too; they are skilled in the art of nonverbal communication and in negotiations with Chinese business people these can be extremely important. Don't interrupt a silence with a clumsy enquiry, "Is everything OK, Mr. Lai?" "You look concerned, Mr. Lai." "You are not saying much, Mr. Lai." This will REALLY annoy him. For him breaking his silence is the height of rudeness.

Your counterparty may say very little in response to your enquiries and will expect you to gather what you need to know from his *gestures* and from the *context* of whatever he says (however little that is). In our more direct Western cultures "virgin negotiators" can find this conduct extremely difficult to work with. But the application here of patience and deductive reasoning can take you a long way. Human communication (as we said before and according to Professor Albert Mehrabian in 1967) is 55% Body language, 38% Tone and just 7% Content anyway, so with a bit of practice it shouldn't be too difficult for you.

Silences and breaks (even long breaks or complete abandonment of negotiations) worry most of us virgin (mostly Caucasian) negotiators. We don't break off discussions or stop talking unless we are deeply offended. However Asian negotiators are often completely comfortable with the idea of dropping a project if they are don't like some part of the negotiation. If this happens, try to go back, identify and then fix the problem.

But one last point; you may be focusing on your potential partner's culture but you mustn't lose sight of them as an individual either. Likeabilty and rapport are key influencers of behaviour simply because we all tend to like people who are "like" us. So it is always best to find out as much as you can about the personalities and communication styles of your counterparties. Then, simply adjust and personalize your approaches according to the individual.

By the way, one note of caution ... this is *not* about attempting to "mimic" foreign accents or for example, trying to match the Japanese social bowing etiquette. You cannot ignore culture – it is impossible – but you must treat it as your backdrop. Because you must also try to focus on the capabilities and manner of the specific individuals at the table.

Attempt to *subtly* "mirror" the person if you can. Lean back when they lean back. Gesture in a similar way. Speak with the same rhythm and level. In short, simply use the same manner of talking and moving. Psychologists also tell us there are basically three ways in which we perceive the world: Visual, Aural and Kinesthetic. We all use a mix of these but one is always dominant and varies according to the individual. *Visual* people see the world in pictures and use words and phrases like: "I see what you mean" ... "I get the picture" ... "Look at it this way." *Aural* (or listening) people view the world primarily in sound form. They use words and phrases such as: "I like the sound of that" ... "I hear what you're saying" ... "That rings a bell". And *Kinesthetic* people perceive the world through touch and sensation. Their common phraseology includes: "That's a bit rough" ... "This feels right to me" ... "It's a rocky road we're riding along now" ... "That makes me edgy". To start the process through which somebody will end up "liking" you (and your ideas) without knowing why, just start using the same type of gestures, looks, sounds, words and phrases that they do.

This is usually successful because a new, mutually, but unconsciously agreed-on, culture is being created just for your efforts.

... and finally

This whole chapter matters because the most persuasive word in the world is "YOU".

If you want other people to be open to the possibility that they might be persuaded by you (a virgin negotiator) then you will get a lot further (faster) if they feel that you are focused on what they want. This is not some new-fangled "New Age" waffle either. Way back in 1936 Dale Carnegie wrote his best selling book *How to Win Friends and Influence People*. (15 million copies in the first 10 years – and still in print today!) In this book, Carnegie says that if you want people to be open to your ideas, then all you have to do is ask them about themselves. So-called "charming" people have simply learnt the power of projecting this "total focus" on the person they are talking to at this particular moment. Why is it so effective? ... because, as with all aspects of social and business persuasion, our primary decisions are made at a deeply subconscious, emotional level. Only when the emotional needs of both you and I are satisfied, will the facts of the case be seriously considered in order to justify a decision to proceed.

What do human beings want? It's not very difficult:

- To feel good about themselves.
- To be listened to.
- To have their values understood.
- To have their culture understood.
- To have their needs understood.

This is what we all want. But of course as humans, the added complication is that we are largely unpredictable. Despite everything that I've written in this chapter so far the person or people you meet at your next negotiation might just act in a way which is totally unpredictable. We get angry, we have egos, we get depressed, we get fearful, we get frustrated. As negotiators we just have to put up with it.

Just remember: not liking someone is not an excuse for not negotiating with them.

How many times do I have to tell you?

Many virgin negotiators don't realize either, that their communication is what goes in at the eyes and ears of the other person (or people) being addressed; it is not at the point that the words come out of their mouths. So they just don't understand that what they say can easily be misinterpreted or may even confuse the other side. It might also go so far as to reinforce prejudices.

So what is the result of this ignorance? A spiral dive in which unintended threats and attacks are perceived and subsequently counterattacked – great fun to watch but very inefficient when we are trying to persuade. The negotiation degenerates into a conflict in which WHO is right becomes more important than WHAT is right. This game of "savingface" is now the important issue rather than the real issues you both originally sat down to negotiate!

If you do not sit down with other people around the negotiating table having previously taken the trouble to assess their sensitivities and continue to be sensitive to any changes in mood, then things can go disastrously wrong. (Don't believe me? ... Consider the endless "Positional" state of world politics ... perhaps the "negotiators" should read this book!)

By the way, this does not mean you have to *give-in* to a tyrant, an aggressive regime or a dominant, power-mad, bullying negotiator ... that would just be *soft* not *sensitive*. Sensitive means acknowledging, listening, considering, asking and being open to the inner consideration with which I asked you to open this book: "maybe he's right".

So set out, at the beginning of any negotiation, to create rapport with the other side. Create an environment in which you and your team and the team on the other side are working together to find a solution to the problem.

SECTION 6

I Don't Know Why I Did That!? (Ploys and "Tricks")

"Whether you think you can ... or you think
you cannot ... ... you're absolutely right"

HENRY FORD

Whenever I open a workshop or seminar on Negotiation I always start by asking the group what they are seeking to gain from the programme. Invariably they all agree that they are looking for some new "negotiating tricks".

Well I don't really DO "tricks".

I know a few bits of dinner table magic and I can make coins come out of children's ears. But using clever word play to get people to do things is not really my cup-of-tea.

The word "tricks" implies conjuring, magic, manipulation and general Machiavellian *chicanery*.

The thing is, if you're seen or thought to be acting sharply by the other side, then you may get away with it *once* but you WILL find it difficult to come back and negotiate on a future occasion.

Don't try this at home (or at the negotiating table)

My own experience is that, for a wise, and efficient outcome, a negotiation requires much more than *Smart Alec* tricks.

I attended an evening seminar in New York a couple of years ago, in which a supposed top-negotiator was going to show us his methods of closing a negotiation in the modern world. His main technique, when things had reached a deadlock, was to suggest that the outstanding issues get written up on a convenient "white board" or flip-chart for all to review. The suggested method went as follows:

The leader of the negotiation stands up with marker pen in hand and writes the numbers 1 to 10 down the left-hand side of the sheet. If there isn't space then at least the numbers 1 to 6 must be written. The instigator of this process must then ask the other side to give him, one-by-one, all the issues still to be resolved; each one is then written next to one of the previously written numbers.

He then asks, after the final issue is written-up, if they are quite sure that is all that remains between them. When the other side agrees that it is, he draws a line across the sheet just below the last issue to be written up. (The seminar leader called this point, "Shutting the list.") The next step is for the leader to say to the group, "So if we can find a way to agree all these points you will go ahead with this deal?"

(This is actually *The Sting*.) They have to say either, "Yes" ... or say there is more to add to the list .... or say "No" and show that they are not really interested (in which case what have they been negotiating about?). They usually say, "Yes". Each point is then addressed with what I can only describe as word-play "objection rebuttal" sales techniques (very 1960s!). I was taught most of them years ago in the highly ferocious copying machine market of the 70s. I am NOT going to lay any of these out here (they are not for today's business world), but as a veteran seller with 37 years' experience I can say that it is more like being hung out to dry by an expert lawyer, in court, than participating in a sophisticated business conversation. The point is that the techniques DO work but usually only once with any given counterparty; next time the same people would be more prepared.

Each time one of the listed points is dealt with the leader must put a line through it and move on to the next one. When all of the points have been covered the leader turns to the group and asks once more, "Is that definitely all?" The luckless "other side" must now say, "Yes", because they have already said, "Yes", at *The Sting* point above. (Saying "No" is tantamount to admitting that they didn't know what they were talking about only a short while before. Humans have a deep, in-built, desire to be consistent.) The contract is then produced and signed leaving the other side wondering what just happened.

I always think of the type of tricky-thing outlined in that New York seminar in terms of a Spanish bullfight. Why do they really have to kill the bull at the end of each bullfight? Why don't they just patch him up and send him back to fight again in a few weeks? Why? … because if they let him back in, next time he'd KNOW!

Likewise if you use "tricks" and clever "word-play" to get what you want, next time (and there is usually a next time) they'll know and be ready for you.

No! … "tricks" are not part of modern negotiating technique.

On the other hand ...

There are some quirks of human psychology that you would do well to consider as a virgin negotiator. These concern the way we all think, the way our brains work and the way we perceive the world.

"Telling" people a whole lot of things is a very poor way of persuading them to do anything. But once you have some notion of how everyone's brain processes information and then instructs us (the human being inhabiting the body) to proceed, you will become a much more persuasive negotiator. You will help people to persuade themselves.

I showed you, right at the front of this book, how you can actually play a trick on your own mind using what psychologists have discovered about the way we all see things. It isn't cold-hard reality; it just helps us to make progress and interpret the world in the safest way possible. This was a terrific way for our brains to help humans perceive the world several hundred thousand, even millions of years ago. This was the time when our subconscious auto-responses were laid down based on the dangerous unprotected desert/jungle world our ancestors lived in. Many of those automatic responses remain however and knowing about them can assist a virgin negotiator to persuade another individual or group to persuade themselves.

You do it to me and then I'll do it ...

The first technique you can employ is that of reciprocation. Deeply imbedded in all our psyches is a need to cooperate and reciprocate. If you do something for me then I will do it to you.

In the animal kingdom primates do it all the time. Male baboons for example form alliances with each other in order that one baboon will distract the Alpha-male, who has monopolized the reproductive females, while the other will copulate with a female. The roles will be reversed later for "payback".

At the negotiating table knowledge of this reciprocation technique can help the virgin negotiator to convince the other party that they are sincere and a worthwhile partner in a transaction. For example, if you find that a particular part of a negotiation is getting tough and you feel there may be a stand-off approaching you will find it extremely useful to break the discussions for a few minutes and take a short break to use the bathroom or get a drink. On your return you should bring with you some small gift. It could be a tray of teas and coffees or a can of soft drink. Even a jug of iced water or some cookies. You offer it first to the other side.

Doing this you will regularly discover that the other side subtly changes its stance. Having received a gift from you affects them at a deeply subconscious level. They now feel a strong desire to reciprocate and return the favour. And the curious thing is that the returned favour may have far greater value than the small gift you brought them.

I read recently of one experiment in which a group of paid volunteers in a university were invited to give their opinions on a series of images presented by the tester. Thinking that this was the whole reason for volunteering they sat through a whole afternoon of opinion giving. Towards the end of the afternoon the tester left the room for a while and returned with a can of soft drink for all. A further hour of wrap-up discussions followed after which the group of volunteers prepared to leave. As they were exiting the tester had a sudden thought! She had just remembered that her daughter had asked her to help with some donations to their school gym team's travelling fund. She asked whether any of the volunteers would like to make a donation. They all gave between $5 and $20 each.

Over several repetitions of the same experiment, some with the final drinks interlude some without (but ALL with the request for donations) it was discovered that the volunteers who had received the surprise gift of drinks, made donations which were in all 80% higher than those who had not.

A simple variation of this theme is to focus on something that you would really like to achieve during the negotiation, but ask instead for something that the other side is almost certain to reject. You must then hold out for it and argue for it for some time. Finally you reluctantly give in (acknowledging the logic of their argument – people love to be "right") and instead make a much smaller or less valuable request (based on your real original interest). The net result is that the other side perceives that your giving-in on a particular point is worthy of reciprocation and you will very often get the lesser request that you really want.

You didn't persuade them ... they persuaded themselves.

This reciprocation thing is big in the human world!

There's not much time left

Well there isn't. We can't stay here in the world for ever. We can't save time ... we can't bank time ... we can't "make" time ... we can only *spend* time. And if you don't spend your allocation of time today then it's gone for ever. All the time in the world is all the time there is in YOUR world.

This feeling that time is getting scarce increases exponentially as you get older. And everybody is aware of it. Things can't last. Don't put off tomorrow what you can do today! "Sale must end Friday!" "Closing Saturday! ... Everything must go!"

Scarcity and the feeling that resources are running out is a great motivator for humans to take action. Real, increasing scarcity of some critical resource (or perception of growing scarcity) is one of the primary reasons for a negotiation in the first place.

In any negotiation it is good to share some information about what you have and what you want but not all of it. If the other side perceives that you have a great deal of what they want, in fact a great deal more than they want, they will generally not think it has much value.

I set a group of Scandinavian executives a negotiating exercise recently in which one side was supposed to own a warehouse which had become grossly overstocked with a particular item which they desperately needed to sell-on. The only alternative facing them at the outset of the exercise was dumping and recycling the articles. Mercifully (for I am a kind god) I presented them with an unexpected buyer desperately seeking just the type of article with which they were overstocked. Instead of endeavouring to find out from the buyer exactly what it was they were seeking and the true value to the buyer, the "selling" side, on hearing their need blurted, "Well I have great news for you ... we have a warehouse FULL of them". And then for the rest of the exercise wondered why the expected price for the articles stayed obstinately low (only just above the recycling price in fact).

My dear virgin negotiator, openness is great and honesty is great. But if you want your counterparty to perceive value in your proposition don't make it too "available". And when you are on the other side and you want something badly, play poker; don't let the other side know your need or the price may well rocket skywards.

Remember the words of American negotiator, Herb Cohen quoted in the first chapter of this book, "I care ... I really *care*! ... but not THAT much!"

"Yes" frames

One thing about humans is that we like to be consistent. If we have said that we will do something on an agreed date and at an agreed time, and especially if we have said it publicly, then we are 80% more likely to do it.

As a trained seller I know that asking someone directly if they would like to proceed with an order or a contract within a few days of meeting them, especially if it is an expensive item, is unlikely to result in a deal. Even if the buyer does buy from me quickly they may reflect and feel that they were pressured. On the other hand if I can encourage a prospective customer to agree with me at various points during the sales process and get them saying "yes" to various ideas, all increasingly harder, then I am much more likely to get them to persuade themselves to buy. None of us wants to feel as if we have been "sold" an idea but we all like to "buy".

So an effective approach for a virgin negotiator is to "take it easy" during the process. Know that a person on the other side of the table who has said, "Yes" to a very small request is much more likely to say, "Yes" to a slightly bigger request and after that "Yes" to a slightly larger one again; they get used to saying "Yes"; "Yes" feels comfortable.

This whole area of self persuasion and "yes" frames was identified in the middle of the 20th century and not by any Western university or academic research but by the Korean Army during the Korean War of the early 1950s. They discovered when talking to American soldiers they had captured and placed in POW camps, that it was relatively easy to get them to begin to turn round their whole political outlook over a few weeks by asking a series of "Yes frame" questions.

The first one was, "Do you think it is *possible* that the American government has ever made a mistake?" The obvious answer from nearly all the soldiers was enough to begin to sow the grain of doubt. Successive simple creative questions over the following weeks encouraged a substantial shift in outlook of even the most hardened soldier.

Power and authority

Throughout the modern business world there are hundreds and thousands and millions of "managers". In fact I don't know many executives who are not senior managers, managers, junior managers, assistant managers or trainee managers. So called "badge engineering" encourages people to believe that they are "making progress". But the great global shortage is not of "managers" but of *leaders*.

The world is hungry for leaders ... leaders who act in a powerful, inspirational and authoritative manner. Nobody on this planet today actually knows what is going to happen in the next few days, months or years. But individuals who seem to know or who appear to have a plan and who can inspire others are in great demand. Empowerment training courses are over subscribed. Leadership programmes run by top universities are full.

Human beings in general look up to powerful authority figures. They admire and are greatly influenced by power. And power or rather the perception of power in negotiations is also extremely influential. But power is not something you're given ... it is something people perceive in you. To paraphrase Henry Ford (founder of the Ford Motor Company), "If you think you *have* power ... or if you think you *don't have* power ... you're absolutely right".

In Robert Ringer's best selling 1970s book, *Winning Through Intimidation*, which is about learning to negotiate in the US real estate market, he tells many tales of his early days as a broker arriving at a counterparty's office for a negotiation, with a huge retinue of apparent "lawyers" (actually friends) in tow. And of his spending money to hire a Lear jet in order to impress on the other side that he was a "big-shot" ... not used to being pushed around.

A similar tale is told in the movie of a true story, *Erin Brockovich* (2000), where presentation of the appearance of power by a tiny country-attorney's office (office secretaries and clerks sitting at the negotiating table acting the role of a highly qualified legal team) was enough to "influence" a major medical company to drop their bullying tactics and negotiate properly.

In Stanley Miligram's famous experiments conducted in the 1970s he discovered that if an apparent "authority figure" told volunteers to do something (in this case apparently torture an individual to the point of death) then an alarming number of people would do as they were told!

The researchers had predicted, before the American experiment, that only one in a thousand people would do this. But when the authority figure (professor's white lab-coat, graying hair, little beard, glasses, clip board) told them that it was OK to proceed past the shouts and pleading of the "victim" (actually an actor in no real danger at all) and that the volunteers would not get into trouble, then 60% of volunteers (600 out of 1000) did as they were told.

Alarming? Maybe, but true nevertheless. And virgin negotiators must be aware of the impact that their power or perceived lack of power will have on the other side.

And it is not just power residing in people. Power also resides in authoritative looking signs ... we are amazingly influenced by the power of "printed" (sometimes engraved) "signs" and "orders".

When I lived in the USA I particularly recall the famous *Candid Camera* TV show practical joke, which involved placing a sign in the road on the main route into Delaware which read "Delaware Closed". The scene, which has been detailed in many books and articles about power, influence and negotiation, was then secretly filmed. Many cars stopped and the drivers approached the "official" standing next to the sign (actually a TV executive involved with the show) and asked what was happening in Delaware. The man just pointed at the notice and said, "Read the sign!" Worried looking drivers took it at face value and asked when it would re-open. They made no attempt to pass the sign. One man is reported to have told the "official" that he hoped it would open soon as he was worried for the safety of his wife and family who lived there.

The very appearance of written documents, agendas and programmes can have a huge effect on the perception of your power in a negotiation. The paper they are written on for example (one of my Norwegian clients *always* comments on the feel of the paper we use in our business) is very import ant.

I mentioned earlier in this book the huge import ance attached to the "production" of your standard run-of-themill business card in a Chinese or Japanese negotiation: it is *never* produced casually from the top pocket of your suit; *always* offered and received with both hands; *always* considered and read by the receiver, for a few seconds; *always* placed on the table in front of you and if there is more than one person in their team the most senior person's card always goes at the top.

And *don't* do what I saw a senior director of my former employer do during a Japanese negotiation ... casually picking up the Japanese executive's card he started rolling it up while he spoke. Our Japanese counterparty was mortified!

The power of paper, card and signs in general, rests in the fact that we humans place more natural authority and legitimacy in the written word than in the words that we hear.

"Once it is written," our subconscious minds seem to say. "Then it must be official."

So now that you know this, how can you, as a virgin negotiator, make effective and strategic use of the knowledge?

Well, first of all don't leap in and start to get everything written down, printed up and set in concrete at the start of every negotiation. Sometimes it is necessary to retain some flexibility in the early stages. On the other hand I have often found myself negotiating with a person and or a team who are not good at processing verbal information, so having something written down which they can process more slowly can be useful.

Having a relatively sieve-like brain myself I always have to write things down during complex negotiation and see the words (my own words) on paper in order to make sense of everything and sort out the important points.

I am not a great e-mailer but I DO however use email and letters to record the facts of the negotiation as I saw them so that nobody can mis-remember them later. My emails are also "rare" so, in the whole "scarcity" arena outlined earlier in this book, they are perceived by the other side to have more value.

I also endeavour to be the one who writes the minutes remembering the old epithet "He who writes the minutes writes the history".

So here are the various points in the negotiation for which I recommend that you try to get something in "powerwriting" on the table first:

Agendas

I always advise participants in our Negotiating Workshops to be the side that writes and prints the agenda. A typed agenda doesn't take long to prepare and I always make sure it is on top quality paper; sometimes even "glossy". You will find that in the "perception of power" game, most human beings on the other side of the table will follow it once it is in front of them. Yes the other side could have done it too but most people aren't stupid … they are simply too lazy!

Even if they do want to subsequently "adjust" the order of some items, you will find that your agenda provides the general framework which suits the way you want to conduct the proceedings.

Proofs and precedents

I am always ready for challenges to my reasons for taking a particular stance in a negotiation so I try to arrive at the table with as much supportive "written" evidence for each point as I can.

In a recent tussle with an insurance company over the value of a car one of my children had "written off" (it wasn't their fault and they were mercifully unhurt) I was challenged to "prove" the car's value up to the point of the accident. I maintained that it was higher than the offer being made by the assessor twice as much in fact ... several thousand pounds sterling.

They had all the insurance industry rule-of-thumb comparison sheets on their side and various industry second-hand car value books. I had done ten minutes work on the Internet and uncovered five cars, same make and model, same condition and mileage, offered for sale by reputable dealers that day (with pictures) at the price I thought my car was worth. The insurers were not prepared for this "proof"; I would go so far as to say they were genuinely surprised. They paid up the full amount ... double their opening offer.

I also spend a long time between phases of negotiations crafting letters which respond to, or present counter proposals to, the other side. I try to make them very persuasive by discussing the benefits (solutions sought by the other side) contained in my offers whilst, when necessary, indicating what could happen if they cannot be met and they reject them.

Just last week I discussed, on the telephone, a training proposal with a customer based in India who works for a company in which I too was once an employee. The man knows me well and we like and trust each other. All the details of his requirements are clear to me but I have now confirmed them all in a detailed written proposal.

Have I wasted my time?

No. The written proposal gives my offer power and authority. It enables me to present an "official" document, properly laid out in a business-like manner. It details each element of the service I provide. It speaks more than anything about the situation the potential customer has told me exists that we can help solve. The fee at the very end feels justified by the "weight" provided by the written document.

Compare that with my contact quickly telling his colleagues something along the lines of, "I spoke to Bob Etherington ... I told him what we want ... he says he can do it ... and his fee will be £xxx,xxx.xx."

"What?!"

Leverage papers

I shouldn't train my customers so well. One of them now regularly produces lower priced quotations from my competitors whenever we sit down to re-negotiate the sales training contract we have with them. Using written evidence to lever yourself a better deal is really like producing the Letter In Your Back Pocket (LIYBP) (see Chapter 2).

When this happens I have to ask questions to make sure they are comparing like with like and also to ensure they are not making a decision on the basis of price alone. "If it's just price," I say. "Then I'm really not the company you need to talk to." Then with my own LIYBP firmly in my back pocket I prepare (mentally) to leave ... it never comes to that I'm pleased to say.

Agreement in writing

Ever since the fateful loft conversion on my own home (fateful for the builder not me) I have always been first to produce the powerful "initial draft agreement".

I did things right on that first occasion (more by luck than judgment I confess) but it taught me a lesson in getting the agreement on paper as soon as possible. This became the model on which the final negotiations with the builder then went ahead. It was a list of my requirements forged by me. It was up to the builder (the other side in this case) to put in suggested changes. I was clearly perceived as "very reasonable" (I never actually said those words) in the way I accepted the builder's minor modifications. The eventual wriggles and mistakes caused by their attempts to "cut corners" once they got started on the project made me glad I had written my own agreement first.

So try to be first with the draft agreement!

As a final example of the power of the written word this is something that happened to me recently. I arrived in the Marriot Hotel Copenhagen, just before lunchtime, one weekday in mid 2006. The hotel lobby was empty at the time so I asked the concierge if he would watch my bags before I checked-in, while I crossed the road to buy a T shirt to wear in the hotel's health club.

When I returned ten minutes later the same previously empty lobby was jam packed with people at the check out desks. I asked the concierge what was happening and he pointed at the sign behind the desk: "**Check Out 12:00 Midday**". He told me that over 90% of all hotel guests read that sign as if it was one of the "Ten Commandments", and dutifully line up on their departure day desperate to check out before the Noon Armageddon! As a serial hotel-late-check-out-requester I was amazed at this, but he told me it happens nearly every day: the mass of hotel guests from all over the world read the sign, then do as they are instructed without question.

Virgin negotiators should note how this perception of power (or lack of power) alters human behaviour. Then, having considered its implications, you may choose to exercise it in one of two ways:

As a first option you can make sure that you have the look and feel of an authoritative person. Your clothes must speak it as you walk into the room: clean, tidy, well-pressed. If you are negotiating with a group whose culture is "dress-down" rather than "formal suit" then your dress-down outfit must be just as sharp.

In that first few seconds your deportment and smile must say (before you even open your mouth) that here is a person who is used to getting what he (or she) wants. That you are a person familiar with negotiating successful deals. A person who has no need to rush. A person whose slow, steady, lower voice tones show that a leader has just walked in. (Interesting to note that humans associate power with a low slow voice).

To get an idea of what I'm saying go down to your local Video/ DVD rental store and take out the Michael Caine/Steve Martin movie, *Dirty Rotten Scoundrels*. As well as renting out a very funny movie you will see how the character portrayed by Caine (Lawrence Jamieson) trains the character played by Martin (Freddy Benson) to exude and create the impression of power in order to attract rich women. Although it is a comedy film, the instructions and education offered to Freddy cover all the points made in this part of the book.

Body Power

Making sure that you can read another person's body language is as important as controlling your own. Here are some quick bullets to review, practice and inwardly digest.

- If you are standing (I stand-up as often as possible during a negotiation especially if the rest stay seated. It places me in a stronger psychological position ... my eye line being higher than theirs).Then adopt the power stance: feet about 30-35 cms apart. Shoulders back, and neck straight. Arms not folded just hanging comfortably by your side.

- If you enter a room make sure your stance is the same. Smile and walk steadily neither slow nor fast. Men make subconscious decisions about your Alpha status on entry within 15 seconds ... women in about 3!

- If you enter a room make sure your stance is the same. Smile and walk steadily neither slow nor fast. Men make subconscious decisions about your Alpha status on entry within 15 seconds ... women in about 3!

- When seated: sit up straight (remember what your mother told you). Don't lean on anything. Don't tip back on your chair or roll on the table.

- Stay alert by placing both your feet flat on the floor, not wound tensely around each other under your chair.

- If you want the other side to see you as more energetic lean forward, arms open on the table. If you want to appear more relaxed then lean back but don't fold your arms.

- Watch your hands: do not touch your face anywhere from your nose down to your neck whilst you are speaking. Don't touch other people unless you know them *really* well or unless you are shaking their hand. These are all signs received by other humans that you are not telling the truth.

- To maintain their trust keep your hands on display at all times. One regularly observed feature in the behaviour of "charming" people is that they repeatedly show the palms of their hands to others. Keep your hands out of your pockets.

- Avoid giving away any stress you might be feeling through wringing your hands, adopting a praying position or clasping them together until the knuckles go white. It's a bit of a giveaway!

- Your eyes are the window on your soul so do make direct eye contact with the whole group. Make any smile wrinkle your eyes if you can.

- Do not look past someone's shoulder when they are speaking to you. They will think you're not interested ... And you ARE interested ... aren't you?

Your second option is to play down your power. You may still decide to look smart and authoritative but appear to be acting on behalf of someone back at "base" who has the real power; a Head-Honcho high up in Head Office who must be contacted before a final decision can be made. Virgin negotiators will find that this is a technique adopted by many negotiators in the Middle East. It can also provide you with thinking time if you feel that there is any desire from the other side to steamroller you.

I have often adopted this technique on finding myself unexpectedly alone on my side of the table faced with a negotiating "panel" on the other side. Playing down power and authority often works quite effectively when you are on the "buying" side of a negotiation. Here it will often pay you to look a little threadbare.

My multi-millionaire uncle (Uncle Ron – antique furniture dealer and commercial property developer in North London) had a special set of tattered clothing which he always wore to negotiations. He even adopted a different name so that nobody would connect him with the wealthy well-dressed person of similar appearance often seen in polite society in the same area.

External and internal power

As you can see, external power is mostly about your having a strong appearance. If the egotiation is being held on your territory, your working environment is part of your external power. Internal power is having real confidence which is usually based on your prior preparation.

If you ask why are these types of power are so important, I will tell you it is because if your external appearance or internal attitude is perceived to lack power or confidence, you may never get the other side to agree with you.

In summary if you want to increase your external power:

- Keep your negotiating environment appropriate to the situation.
- Make sure you are dressed in a manner which is appropriate to the situation.
- Speak slowly and clearly. Adopt a strong, full voice. The people on the other side of the table must be able to hear you and understand what you are saying before you can come to an agreement.

- To be perceived as powerful, lower your voice and avoid any weak, high-pitched tone.
- Be polite.

To increase your internal power:

- Remember the US military formula "The 6 P's": **P**rior **P**reparation **P**revents **P***** **P**oor **P**erformance. Try a dry run practice more than once. Practice is negotiating's best kept secret ... hardly anybody does it.
- Make sure you have everything on your negotiating flight deck that you think you might need. Then you won't get in a panic. (As aviators say: "It is far better to be *down here* wishing you were *up there* ... than *up there* wishing you were *down here*.")

Finally, although I don't encourage the use of *manipulative "ploys"* (well not many anyway), I hope I have opened your virgin negotiator's eyes to those which may be applied by unscrupulous negotiators on the other side of the table. So should *you* use them yourself now that you know what they are? Aren't they all rather tricky in nature?

Well, in the words of the evil, fictional politician Francis Urquhart, played by Ian Richardson in the 1980s BBC TV series *House of Cards*: "You may *say* that ... but I couldn't *possibly* comment!"

SECTION 7

Unconscious Incompetence and Conscious Competence

Educational psychologists tell us that when we learn new things, we all go through four levels of learning:

1. Unconscious Incompetence.
2. Conscious Incompetence.
3. Conscious Competence.
4. Unconscious Competence.

The lowest level they call *Unconscious Incompetence*. This is the level in which you don't know what it is you don't know so, in your innocence, you behave as you have always behaved not knowing whether you are behaving in the most effective way or not.

The "*Conscious Competence*" phase is the one, just before the final phase (*Unconscious Competence*) in which you now know and understand how to behave but have to think about it every time because it isn't yet a good natural habit.

Unconscious incompetence

As a virgin negotiator there are a number of unfortunate very common behavioural mistakes made by most negotiators. These are very well described by the phrase, *Unconscious Incompetence*.

Under this heading there are four bits of behavioural advice which average negotiators should heed (but rarely do).

They are:

1. Never **argue with an angry man**.
2. Don't: "**behonestwithyou**".
3. Eliminate: "**an interesting idea but** ..."
4. Avoid: "**and another point** ..."

Let's look at them one by one.

Never argue with an angry man

It can be great fun to watch a huge row develop during a negotiation but it is rarely fun to be in the middle of it. A shouting vindictive argument might be quite satisfying for a bullying personality but it is rarely persuasive. You might just *feel* better because you were able to "have a go at" or "score points" off the people opposite but all your attacking them won't change their minds. And you are not there to prove that you are "right".

The four levels of learning

1. **Unconscious incompetence**

Imagine you're a member of a remote jungle tribe. You've never seen a motor car before, indeed you don't know that motor cars even exist. If this is the case you don't know that you cannot drive a motor car. You are an "Unconscious Incompetent".

2. **Conscious incompetence**

One day you hear a noise and through the jungle thicket comes a large metal object with wheels. Inside the frame is a man. The large metal object stops outside your village. You join other members of your village and gather round the object. The smiling man inside the object opens a door and steps out giving sweets and trinkets to the gathered throng. He lets you look inside the object ... he points at it and says, "Kar". You see a seat inside the "Kar"; he indicates that you may sit on the seat. You sit inside and wait for the "Kar" to move again. It stays where it is. You realize now there is a thing called a "Kar" and that it "goes along" but you don't know how to make it do that. You are now a "Conscious Incompetent".

3. **Conscious competence**

The smiling man (who miraculously speaks your language) asks you if you'd like to learn to make the car "go along". He then spends several days showing you how to steer it, stop, start, reverse and go forwards. You start to understand how to do it but there's a lot to learn and it takes several weeks to get in the swing of it. You have to consciously think of each necessary move you have to make. You are becoming a "Conscious Competent".

4. **Unconscious competence**

After a month or so you have moved on. You discover that you can take other members of your tribe for a ride in the "Kar". While you are making it "go along" you can easily talk to the other people riding with you while, at the same time, controlling its progress. "Driving the Kar" has become a habit you no longer have to actively think about. You have achieved a behaviour change. You are now an "Unconscious Competent".

In the English parliament every Wednesday whilst the parliament is sitting, there is a televised ritual called "Prime Minister's Question Time". During this ritual Members of Parliament can ask the Prime Minister of the day questions on his government's current policies.

Regular viewers (and it is shown on TV all over the world including USA) will know that it often develops (or should I say "degenerates") into a shouting match between the main opposition parties and the government; this is mainly conducted through the leaders of the main parties.

This exchange is closely watched by key journalists who judge the winners and losers at any PMQs on their knock about robustness; how fast can one side "rebut" the taunts of the other side. How can one side "top" the claims of the other with counter claims of their own?

An attack from one side produces a defence and counter attack from the other who in turn must defend and then attack back. The downward spiral continues until they run out of steam. Does it change anyone's opinion? Of course not.

Arguing with an angry man is like throwing paraffin on a fire ... it simply makes things worse.

Don't: "behonestwithyou"

Many people in business, not just "virgin" negotiators, pepper their "persuasive" chatter with *behonestwithyous*. "Well to be perfectly honest with you ..." "To be truthful here ..." "I'm going to be straight with you at this point ...".

The first point here of course is that throwing in a "behonestwithyou" has the opposite effect to the intended one. Far from underlining your forthright honesty towards the other side, it makes your counterparties ask themselves, "So you haven't been honest with us up to now then?"

Most average negotiators then go on to add something like, "we are making you a really excellent offer here" or "this is a very fair proposition on our part" or "you have to agree this is a great deal for you".

These, once again, have the "paraffin on the fire" effect. Because rather than making the people opposite say, "... well now you point out how fair you're being we fully agree and can see what a great counterparty you have turned out to be." They actually find themselves thinking, "... so by telling us that THEY are being fair and reasonable they are implying that we are NOT being fair and reasonable!" So, the act of telling your negotiating counterparty about your generosity towards them is not an efficient or effective way of persuading them. It actually has exactly the opposite effect.

Eliminate: "an interesting idea but ..."

Most people in business have not learnt that one of the key skills of communication and persuasion is "listening". Researchers tell us that most individuals listen only to the first three words on average of any statement spoken by someone else. Instead of listening, people are thinking about their response. They are just waiting for their turn to talk! To be a good listener, takes discipline and concentration. I read in two UK daily newspapers recently (the *Guardian* and the *Daily Telegraph*) that there is such a shortage of people prepared to listen to what other people have to say, that there is a new profession called "Professional Listener". These people are not psychoanalysts or psychiatrists they just sit there and pay full attention to anybody who has something they want to say.

In negotiation you MUST be seen to be listening to ALL the other side's proposals however crass or stupid you may believe them to be. Humans (as we have already discussed) value the words that come out of their own mouths very highly ... much more highly, in fact, than anything anybody else tells them (including YOU).

So if we react to a proposal made by the other side by immediately tabling one of our own ("yeah ... *an interesting idea but* **we'd** like to suggest ..."), instead of being seen to take time (minimum ten minutes as a rule of thumb) to discuss and show interest in their prior suggestion, we should not be surprised to find them largely unresponsive. In short other humans are most closed to OUR ideas if they have just presented one of their own.

A negotiation is not like a typical family party in which everyone is talking and nobody's listening. A negotiation is an exchange of ideas and proposals all of which MUST be heard and seen to be heard. For this reason and as a self confessed serial talker (and a still learning professional listener), I always write a reminder at the top of my negotiating note pad: *"Maybe they're right."*

Avoid: "and another point ..."

Why do so many learner-persuaders in business believe that a lot of stuff, a load of features, a pile of arguments and stacks of supporting points is persuasive? A big pile of things simply doesn't persuade. A weight of arguments designed to show that "you are right", doesn't ever do the trick in negotiation ... sorry. And yet with so many people out there in business land who have attended university and who were taught to support their various pieces of written work, theses and essays with many "arguments" this is not easy to accept. I heard the US based sales skills writer and lecturer Neil Rackham once say in a talk that, although he didn't like tricky ploys in negotiation, there was one that he had seen used very effectively against people with a higher education (like the people I just described). He said that, during a negotiation, if a bright (and higher educated) person across the other side of the table raises an objection to a proposal from your side, it can be quite effective to ask, "Is that the only thing that concerns you?" And the "bright" person, having been taught that more (arguments) is better, will invariably say, "Well there's something else too and it's this ... blah blah blah."

If you then say ... "And is *that* all?" They will generally add something else to the list: "And of course there is also ... blah blah blah". The art is to keep this going for a couple more rounds. The interesting thing is that each successive supporting argument from the bright person will, usually, be successively weaker. Finally a point will be reached at which the argument is so weak that you can react, e.g. "If I could just take you up on that. Are you really saying that you can't accept our proposal because it is 'less' expensive than our original offer?"

The important thing to remember about persuasive "supporting arguments" is to find just one or two and then stick to them. Simple as that.

Conscious competence

On the other hand there are a few other behaviours that really effective negotiators use all the time. As a virgin negotiator you will find that, at first, you will have to *concentrate* on using these properly every time; in this phase of learning you will be using *Conscious Competence*. But with a bit of regular conscious practice you will find your negotiations becoming increasingly efficient, en route to Unconscious Competence (= top negotiator *habit*).

Never make a statement when you could ask a question

Just before he died, the British comedian and satirist Peter Cook (once part of a double act with the late, diminutive film star Dudley Moore) made one last comedy appearance on a BBC TV show. He acted the part of a typical professional soccer manager (Alan Latchley) being interviewed by the real TV presenter Clive Anderson. It was typically hilarious and very well observed. When Anderson asked Latchley to tell him the secret of successful soccer management he replied with no small amount of fervour and passion: "Motivation!" "Motivation! Motivation! Motivation! ... the three '**M**s'!"

The business world is full of these and similar aphorisms, some daft and contrived, others quite accurate. In the more serious real world of property selling, for example, most experts will tell you that experience shows that it is actually, "Location, Location, Location" that dictates the desirability of a residential property. Likewise, when it comes to the real world of Negotiation, experience shows that there is an essential three word mantra there too. In this case it is: "the three '**I**s'!" "**I**nformation! **I**nformation! **I**nformation!"

A key tool for all negotiators is contained in the amount of prior investigation you are able to do into the interests of the other side. If you can't find out much then use your intuition and imagination to best-guess what they might be. If you were in their shoes what do you *think* they might be looking for? The more "intelligence" you can gather *before* you sit down at the table the better. Once you are in the negotiation, be alert to all the signs and unconscious signals that all humans find difficult to conceal. Always be seeking more information. Ask questions. Never make a statement when you could ask a question. If they ask YOU a question try to find out *why* they asked it.

"So you're asking if you can have it on a 2 year lease-back contract? Can you tell us how that would help you?"

"That's an interesting question: *could we train **all** your people*? Well if we are able to provide training for all of them instead of just the first ten what would that mean to you?"

I recall two negotiation problems in this area in my own "virgin negotiator" days.

My failure to ascertain why a counterparty was querying something before answering, resulted in a couple of difficult situations. One was during a negotiation for the sale of a number of large copying machines to a local government office in London; my biggest-ever sale up to then! The negotiator on the buying side suddenly asked me, "Mr. Etherington are these machines of yours very heavy?" "Oh no!" I spluttered. "Compared with other equivalent manufacturers machines, ours weigh very little!" "Oh dear ... that's not good news," said the man. "We want heavy machines here ... if they are lightweight we've found that our staff tend to wheel them round to be adjacent to their own workstations. Perhaps we need to have a rethink about this deal after all!"

On another occasion I was negotiating with an American bank in New York to sell them an electronic trading system for 200 of their currency dealers. The system would enable them to transact multimillion-dollar deals at the push of a button. I was asked, during the final stages of the proceedings, whether it was "easy to use?" "Yes very easy," I said (fingers crossed). "Very easy indeed!" "Ah ... really!" said the Head of Trading. "Which presents us with a problem! If it IS that easy, we are going to be faced with the same problem that I heard Bank XXXX faced last week when a trader, fiddling with the keyboard, accidentally traded several million dollars worth of bonds! No we need a service which is not so VERY easy to use!" Unbelievable but true; my too-fast answer to his question had triggered a warning bell in his head. Always try to find out why they are asking a particular question. Always be seeking more information, information, information!

And remember, that questions are far more persuasive than statements in every part of the business environment.

Regularly re-check progress

In the early1980s I was a London based junior sales executive for the international news agency Reuters. I was tasked with selling their growing range of sophisticated electronic financial trading systems for professional money market dealers. One of my prospective clients was a Middle Eastern bank who we dearly wanted on board because they would potentially be able to trade a wide range of foreign exchange prices with European and American banks. In the London financial markets of the 70s and 80s foreign exchange trading was THE big profit market. My London contacts were very keen to go ahead but told me I had to travel to Bahrain very soon to speak to the "big-boss".

I "sold" the idea of the trip to my boss, got permission and booked my British Airways flight (alas – "ha-ha" – it had to be in First Class; all other sections being sold out) and off I went to Bahrain to "negotiate". I was there for a whole week, explaining to various nodding ranks of senior Arabian bankers, what such a London-centred, foreign exchange trading deal on the Reuters network would mean to them. For most of the time they sat silently, politely nodding, whilst I continued yapping and presenting my case for their foreign exchange price participation.

On the last day, Thursday, four days after my arrival, I finally stopped talking. I asked the big-boss a question ... just about my first question of the week!

I said, "So, Mr. Zubari, do you have any questions?"

"Yes, Mr. Etherington," he replied. "We have ... errrrr ... *one* question!"

"What is it, Mr. Zubari?" I asked.

"We ... don't ... *understand*."

"I'm sorry ... what is it that you don't understand, Mr. Zubari?"

"Anything," he replied. "We don't understand *anything*!"

After four full days we were apparently still at "square one". I was flabbergasted, but what could I do? Did they not understand English perhaps? There was no time to go back over my week's work. It was late on Thursday afternoon. I spluttered a few attempts at what I thought were appropriate "probing" questions but the moment was past. They had all mentally "left the room" and gone home. My car to the airport arrived and a polite cohort (one of the big-boss's negotiating team) was provided to accompany me on the journey across the causeway to the airport.

Curiously the conversation about the possible foreign exchange deal resumed in the car, with my host conducting his end of it in perfect English ... it appeared that he had understood a lot more than "nothing" with regard to my proposal. Actually at least *he* seemed to have understood "everything". However there were clearly a few "issues" to sort out which (he felt) he and I could do during the car ride. It may not come as a surprise to you that we did end up agreeing a deal during that journey. However with my host's pretty shrewd assessment of my position at that point (young ambitious executive salesman ... sent quite a way around the world like a knight-on-a-white-charger ... very expensive roundtrip flight ticket ... expensive week in a hotel in expensive oil-city ... the ever shortening time left in this car journey to retrieve something from this exercise ... my boss in London expecting great news from me) who do you think ended up with the better part of the deal? You've guessed it!

Yet had I "known then what I know now", it could have turned out really differently. Had I been taught (back then) that "regular progress checks and agreements-so-far" during a complex negotiation, are the hallmarks of a top negotiator it wouldn't have gone so wrong. Had I realized that regular "summarizing" was the key, it would have been *rather* (no "*very*") difficult for them to pull the "we don't understand" ploy at the very end.

This apparent failure to understand or reconfirm assumed agreements because of a failure of the other side to regularly summarize progress, is a favourite move of many tricky negotiators. Yet if you have taken the trouble to do it, then you stay in a controlling position. It becomes harder, whenever the reality is that you do hold the weaker hand, for them to manufacture a false deadline and pressure you, as the Bahrain banker successfully pressured me into accepting a less good deal.

"Because" before you snap

One reason that "questions" are a top seller's favourite tool is that when a prospective counterparty is answering your question their brain is fully occupied processing the answer. They cannot, at the same time, be processing an objection to any proposal the seller may have made. In a similar way a top negotiator also uses questions to focus and control the progress of a negotiation. However another important way to keep control is when you need to turn down or object to some proposal made by the other side. A virgin negotiator may think that if someone on the other side puts forward a "ridiculous" suggestion that is just not acceptable, the best response would be to let them know immediately – in no uncertain terms – that it can't be done!

However if you watch an experienced and successful negotiator at work then you will find that there is no such instant rebuttal. In fact at no time will this experienced negotiator let anyone on the other side have any warning that they are about to raise an objection or disagree in some way. Instead they will spend some time detailing some facts about their side's position including those bits of salient background information that will help them understand. Only when a full explanation has been given will they then add that those are the reasons they cannot agree to their proposal.

For example: "If I understand you correctly you're asking for a contract which is one year long? So if I may, I'd like to explain about our business approach. Our service is fully bespoke and individually crafted to provide you with exactly what you need. All our trainers are nationals in the countries that you have selected. So that we can provide your staff with the type of full training programme you have requested – as opposed to a simple one-off two-day training course which you said you do not want – we need to ensure that our trainers are themselves fully trained. This normally takes 3–4 months and takes place in our New York office. Once this is done they are ready to return and begin delivering the programme for you, locally, in modules spread over 9–12 months. This means that any programme is probably not going to be completed inside 12 months even if we were to start today. Also some of your people will, as you have said, require a longer period and further reinforcement. So for this reason we have set the minimum contract period for all our bespoke training to two years rather than the one year you mentioned."

This approach ties in very nicely with a surprising quirk of human psychology which is that other humans are much more likely to acquiesce and go along with our requests if we provide them with a simple explanation for making them in the first place. I have revealed this little gem to many corporate audiences and always get the response, "That would never work on me!!"

For instance, one example I give is that if you are ever waiting in line for something and would like to get to the front quickly then, you might think, that announcing some emergency on your part would increase the chances of your being let through. However, you will find that, provided you give a reason to the people in front of you, then you are 80% more likely to be allowed to the head of the line emergency or not.

To prove the point, one sceptical group of executives in Norway were attending a recent workshop led by me entitled, "Assertiveness and Influence". They were very polite – as Norwegians in general are – and their boss felt that other people in the company were taking advantage of their desire to please. They were consequently over burdening his team with work which, he said, had to stop. So, at lunchtime, I decided to prove that this particular technique was effective. I told them that we were about to break and that I wanted them all to go down to their company restaurant and do something very un-Norwegian.

I asked each of them to go straight to the front of one of the "hungry" self-service queues (it is always chaotic and longlined particularly at the start of lunchtime – this is a very large company) and say exactly these these words: "Would you let me through to the counter please because I need to get some food."

You might think that if they had said, "... because I have to leave immediately after lunch to get to the airport" or "...because I have a meeting with the Managing Director in ten minutes" their chances would be improved ... but no. Simply giving voice to a reason (the same reason everyone else was standing there) for their request was enough to be admitted to the front. In fact, in this case, 100% of the 14 participants in my Assertiveness and Influence Workshop reported that they had been let in!

I'm (sort of) ashamed to admit that I have also done this to get to the front of the long zigzag security check-in line at airports around the world ("... because I have to get a flight") and also to the front of the line in Post Office queues in London and New York ("... because I have to post a parcel"). You might ask what would happen if everyone did this. Well ... they don't and they won't. They read or hear about the technique and then convince themselves that it just won't work so they never use it.

But, virgin-negotiator that you are, I offer a variation of it to you: always give the people on the other side of the table your reasons then tell them that is why you cannot accept their proposal ... it works.

Use information as currency

Most amateur negotiators believe that telling the other side too much about your business interests is not a good or profitable way to conduct a negotiation. Certainly telling your co-negotiators too much ("You say you are desperate to buy 100,000 copies of J.R. Hartley's 1975 book on fly-fishing technique. Well you've come to the right place ... we have a warehouse full of them which we are very keen to shift!") is going to give you a big problem if you expect to be able to sell them at a high price.

On the other hand not telling them anything about your situation and what you are trying to achieve during your negotiation, may restrict their ability to assist you to get there. Therefore it is a good idea to have a think about what information you are willing to trade during the negotiation. Experienced negotiators trade increasingly "personal" questions with the other side in order to find out how much they can trust the people they are facing and also to gain more information about the other side's interests.

"OK you've asked us to detail our likely ordering sequence if this deal goes ahead (which we've done) and you have requested a list of our existing clients who also use this service (which we have also done). Now *before* we answer your last question (on the subject of which other potential partners we may be approaching on this project), we would like you to answer a couple of questions that we have and in the same amount of detail." (i.e. *"You show me yours and I'll show you mine."*)

A virgin negotiator also needs to know that (unlike the way I recommend you handle an objection – as detailed in the previous section) it often pays to sound a big warning bell during a negotiation, that an important question is on its way: "Ladies and gentlemen something is worrying us a bit here and John, we would really like to ask YOU a couple of questions at this point. And John we hope your answers will clarify the situation. The questions are these ... firstly how experienced are your telesales marketers in selling our type of product and secondly which of your existing large customers can we talk to who will testify to your abilities?"

Hanging a big sign on your important questions and shouting: "here comes a question" has the very dramatic effect of concentrating the minds and thoughts of everyone in the room on John and his answer(s). It means that John and his team have to provide a truthful answer which will inevitably be remembered by all who were there. If he doesn't he knows that it will come back to haunt him at a later stage in the project.

SECTION 8

Putting it All Together

"This calls for a very special blend of
psychology and extreme violence!"

VYVYAN (ADRIAN EDMONDSON)
1980S BBC TV SERIES *THE YOUNG ONES*

A negotiation is rather like parallel railway tracks carrying steam locomotives driven by "our side" on one track and the "other side" (or "other sides") on the other track. If our separate locos are travelling in the same direction and doing so without needing assistance in the shape of coal, water, drivers or firemen from the other side, there is no need for a negotiation. We will all get where we need to go without any help.

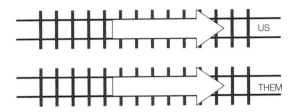

No negotiation required

If our two locomotives are on parallel tracks but travelling in completely opposite directions there is nothing we can do and no chance of any co-operation.

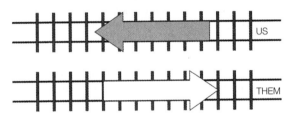

No negotiation possible; going in opposite directions.
No chance to assist each other

A negotiation is only possible when we are travelling in the same direction as our counterparty(ies) with us able to offer help and assistance to them. And they are able to offer complementary help and assistance to us.

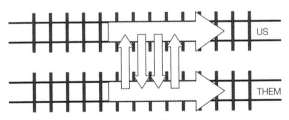

All real negotiations look like this diagram

In a real negotiation we share a common interest in moving forward to our individual destinations. The negotiation sets up a framework for agreement to work together in certain areas for at least part of the journey. In the case of the locomotives above, our side might be able to bargain with them to let them have a driver and coal and they might let us have a fireman and some water.

It is worth noting that if we have something they want and there is no other way to get it apart from us and we need little or nothing from them (except their money) then we probably won't negotiate and we'll just sell it to them.

So whilst a negotiation may (and usually does) include some exchange of money there will usually be other things included which may be exchanged as part of the final agreement.

Therefore to *negotiate* we must have the ability to adjust the various elements which are available to bargain over. And this may occasionally be a little painful because *our* immediate needs may be out of step with *theirs*. So while we DO want to cooperate, accommodating the other side's needs may at the same time present us with difficulties.

For example, to keep the tortuous locomotive analogy going for just a bit longer, the slower "freight" locomotive would like the passenger express to slow down a little so that the exchange of resources can take place. And the passenger express would like the freight train to increase speed to keep up with them. This can be frustrating, yet they both have a common goal in finding ways to cooperate because who knows when they may need to work together in the future on the same parallel railway track.

Cooperation and "The Prisoner's Dilemma"

Realizing the value of human cooperation is at the heart of successful negotiation. "The Prisoner's Dilemma" is a well known philosophical exercise used by most of the world's business schools in order to set students thinking about the advantages and disadvantages of cooperation in business.

The situation presented to the students is as follows: two well-known felons are arrested by the police on suspicion of committing a crime. They are placed in separate cells and each presented with the following proposition. "We are quite sure that you two committed the crime but we have no proof. But if you tell us that your 'colleague' did it alone then we will put him in prison for ten years and release you without charge. But if he tells us that you did it and that he had nothing to do with it then you will go to prison for ten years and he will be released. If you both deny doing it then we will have to release both of you. Yet if you both admit it was a joint job then you will both go to prison for just one year. So what's it to be?"

Once they have discussed "the dilemma" the students are invited to play a game generally called "Red/Blue". In "Red/Blue" the class is split into two groups and acts out "the dilemma" with two cards per team; one red and one blue.

The tutor is very careful to announce at this point that the object of the game is to achieve a positive score.

The game is played over ten rounds and begins when the tutor asks each group to tell him (quietly) whether they want to play Red or Blue. Once the individual teams have revealed their opening choice, out of eye or earshot of the other team, the tutor reveals the choices and scores as follows:

- If both teams have chosen red then they both get –200 points.
- If both teams have chosen blue then they both get +100 points.
- If team A have chosen blue and Team B have chosen red then A gets –200 points and B gets +200.

- If team A have chosen red and Team B have chosen blue then A gets +200 points and B gets –200 points.
- The points gained in each successive round are added to each team's cumulative total.
- From the fourth round the two teams may confer (negotiate) about their intended actions in the next round.
- From the eighth round (inclusive) the teams must confer before each round.

What generally happens is that, despite the tutor's early statement that, "*the objective of the game is to achieve a positive score*", at least one of the teams makes it their objective to win each round (at the expense of the other side). This happens despite frequent conferring enforced from round eight. The teams DO confer and come to a verbal agreement, then – lo and behold – at least one plays a *completely different card* from the one agreed during the previous conference. This may leave one side ahead but the other side justifiably feels let down and lied to *which is exactly what has happened*. So they too now start to look out only for their own interests and try to mislead the other side and, from then on, the whole game deteriorates. Too late they all, finally, heed the tutor's "positive score" objective and attempt to reverse out of their downward spiral in about round seven.

It is living proof that, for relationships in business which need to endure for more than one deal, co-operation and honesty are the keys.

By the way don't play this game at family parties ... you may never speak to your close relatives ever again!

So how does a virgin negotiator prepare to use all the material laid out in the first seven chapters of this book, in order to enter and then emerge from a cooperative negotiation with a win-win or as near win-win as it is possible to get?

Much of the negotiation activity that I get involved in (both "training" and actively "doing") is at the "top end"; mainly in the international money and energy markets. In both these industries it is normal for senior management to impose on the negotiating team certain limits on each bargain-able item. This naturally restricts how far we are allowed to adjust them during the negotiation. As I said in Chapter 2 this mandate is often preceded, these days, with a demand for the negotiating team to present a practical Plan B (or LIYBP). So this leads, initially, to the need for an internal negotiation with all the departments concerned, in order that everyone is "on board" before the negotiating team sits down for the external negotiation.

The rules and tools are exactly the same for the internal and external negotiations but the internal negotiations are often much more difficult. In these, success is often down to your persuasive presentation skills (unashamed plug: read my book *Presentation Skills for Quivering Wrecks* for guidance) as opposed to your negotiation skills. This is because company policy and real cost cutting restricts the ability of department heads to help you, without falling foul of "internal politics".

About 20 years ago I went "outside my mandate" (Oh horror!) when charged to come up with an international sales competition prize for a well known financial information company who was my employer at the time. During "negotiations" I had gone ahead and hired the Carribean holiday-home island of a well known international entrepreneur, for a sum somewhat outside my agreed budget. Not only that, I had no agreement from the various area managers for Europe, USA, UK, Middle East and Asia to even go ahead with this particular prize. The Managing Director apparently "went mad" when he found out during an area manager's meeting the following week. Still "mad" he then telephoned me in London and tore into me verbally for 15 minutes, calling me all the names under the sun. As a result I honestly thought that my employment was about to be terminated. However all of a sudden, and much to my surprise, he stopped. "Right," he said. "Bollocking over ... well done!!"

I was stunned. Clearly the company politics dictated that he needed to be on record as having given me a sound thrashing for my misdemeanour. However my action, whilst "outside the mandate" was clearly thought by him, on reflection, to be the correct one under the circumstances; so I got off, "Scott free". My guardian angel must have been watching over me that day!

The problem is that none of us negotiators can count on such fortuitous circumstances every time we break a mandate. After my little incident, outlined above, I began to take much more care in securing my mandates compared with my other negotiating colleagues in the company and it paid dividends (I was, after all, now a marked man in the company). As a result I was never in such a potentially bad position again.

So I advise you, if your negotiations are at the top end of the negotiating spectrum and require internal mandates, then spend a lot of time on the detail. Work hard, internally, to get exactly the mandate you want so that you don't have to resell your negotiation after the event.

The four initial pre-preparation steps:

1. Decide exactly what it is you want to achieve and why they should negotiate with you ... and why you should negotiate with them.
2. State clearly the elements of your LIYBP (Chapter 2).
3. If you need a negotiating mandate from your superiors, then get one but do your best to make sure it is the best and most wide ranging one you can get away with.
4. Make up your mind (with the whole of your "Aspirational" negotiating team) that you are willing

to cooperate with the other side and if necessary, vary some of your selected business terms during the negotiations. (You can't just sit there insisting on all your standard terms!)

Once you have done that, the next part of your preparation is to take a piece of paper and do a straightforward S.W.O.T analysis (**S**trengths **W**eaknesses **O**pportunities and **T**hreats), the basic work-tool of so many project management training programmes.

Here's an example. Let's say we are a large timber (lumber) wholesalers. There is currently a world shortage of wooden fencing panels (actually true in the early 21st century) and our own customers are desperate to get hold of some. Our normal Norwegian suppliers are about to sit down with us in London to negotiate a supply contract for the next few months.

Our S.W.O.T analysis is shown below. If you take the trouble to sit down and think it through rather than "hope" it will all work out, you will often be nicely surprised at how many weaknesses you can think of in the other side's position. This can reinforce your feeling of confidence before you get to the table.

In addition it will help you consider some of the possible unexpected developments that could be happening: have they got plenty of potential customers in this tight market? Has there been any problem with the lack of any really cold winters in that part of Norway for several years – does it affect fir tree growth? All things you need to check.

S.W.O.T analysis for negotiation

Power at the negotiating table isn't something anyone can give you. Power and confidence is something you feel first inside and then project, make sure you have all the information you can gather especially when it comes to listing your own strengths.

	Strengths	Weaknesses	Opportunities	Threats
US	We are a very large client of theirs if not THE largest in the UK	We really require this deal as they have access to the largest pine forest resource in the world	We may be able to introduce them to some of our North American associate companies	If we fail some of our regular customers will go elsewhere
	Once this temporary shortage is past there may be too much fencing timber around. They need to keep us happy so that we buy	We have nobody else in mind who can supply us quickly	They know that we always pay their invoices in less than 30 days. They never have to chase us now or in the future	They may find another company willing to pay more
THEM	In a tight market they can supply us very quickly	Certainly once the current shortage is over there will be an oversupply and the prices will drop sharply	If they keep us happy on this deal we could well open up opportunities for them to supply us with other raw timber we traditionally buy elsewhere	If they lose our custom on this they may think we will be upset and then they'll have to find other customers who will spend as much with them as we do
	They might guess that we have nowhere else to go for these panels at the moment	Does lack of snow or general global warming affect fir tree growth and their profits? Better find out before		Any alternative customer to us might turn out to be an unreliable payer

No personal or business life is free of problems. We all have them. But for some reason we all think that our problems and weaknesses are greater than those of the other side. Putting yourself in the other side's shoes during the planning phase can help you see the problems they might have. With that and your Plan B (LIYBP) you will always feel less pessimistic and much more confident.

Some of the areas you will find it useful to incorporate in your S.W.O.T analysis are:

- The availability or otherwise of the things being negotiated over.
- The competition for those things.
- The changes likely to affect the market (nothing stays the same).
- The importance of the outcome to you and (your guess) to the other side.
- Your past relationship with the other side.
- How urgently you or they need the deal.

Now you're ready to prepare and plan

So your S.W.O.T analysis has provided you with a big pile of information. But as we discussed in Chapter 3, a big pile of facts and numbers sprayed at the other side is not a very persuasive strategy.

In the very first negotiation workshop that I was asked to lead in the oil industry, one of the geologists on the programme said that his normal negotiating strategy was to dump all his words and requirements on the other side and get out as soon as possible. He told me that he hated the bargaining process. He was a true virgin negotiator. It took me over a week to prove to him that a lot of facts on their own are not persuasive.

Effective negotiators, once they have accumulated their information always consider first HOW they are going to use it.

As usual, in a book like this, we use a mnemonic at the preparation stage and being a closet pessimist I have a great one of my own which makes sure I take time to do the preparation properly.

The word is "GLITCH". And without using a GLITCH I have run into plenty!

Goal – What are you trying to do in this negotiation?

LIYBP – What's your Plan B?

Impale priorities – What are your absolute priorities? The ones you MUST nail?

Targets – What are your targets and limits for each of your variable items ?

Concessionary costs – How much will any concessions cost you?

Heart – Do you really have the heart (Aspiration and Attitude) to get the best deal?

1. SO WHAT IS YOUR **G**OAL?

Read any self-help book and they will tell you that the way to get what you want is to know exactly what you want at the start. Most people don't even know what their goal is for this week, this month or this year let alone for their whole life or an upcoming negotiation. Knowing exactly what you want is actually quite difficult for quite a lot of people. Without this clear objective at the front of your mind it is very easy even for highly intelligent people to emerge from a negotiation with something they didn't want! (See the earlier workshop example given in this book of auctioning a $50 bill for $54 or more!)

The toughest thing for a negotiator is setting your goal at just the right level. A goal such as, "To get the best price we can" is far too woolly. Or a goal like, "To get agreement for a minimum 20 days training at a minimum of £1900 per session and no further discounts if they want anything less than 40 days and full payment if any session is postponed or cancelled less than one week beforehand" is far too detailed and is simply a list of targets. It leaves no room for any bargaining.

A much more realistic way for a virgin negotiator to proceed with Goal Setting is to use the "**Weneedbecause**" model so that your goal reminds you of the overall goal once you get to the table and states what the larger benefit of this will be.

We need to get an obvious win-win in this negotiation **because** this client will still employ us if the predicted industry recession transpires next year.

We need to get this deal with Aligator Oil **because** we will be seen by other people in the industry as credible consultants.

We need to come to an agreement today even if it means a profit-share **because** this company is aiming to dominate the conference market in the next five years and the potential for us partnering with them is huge.

We need to maintain the current income level from them **because** any change would create a precedent and we will offer them, in return, wide ranging flexibility and cancellation rights within their global contract because they are an excellent customer.

Once you are clear on your "Goal" you should check your S.W.O.T chart and see whether anything needs adding especially with regard to the other side's possible or probable points of view. In particular what might the "Letter In *Their* Back Pocket" look like. If you were them what alternatives would you have if this negotiation doesn't work out? Once you have formed an idea of this you will want to think in advance how you might be able to weaken it!

2. LETTER IN YOUR BACK POCKET

I'm not going to repeat the whole of Chapter 2. However the true power balance at the table usually comes down to how much you or "they" need to do the deal. The more you can say to yourself (like Herb Cohen quoted in Chapter 2) "I care! ... I really care! ... but not that much!" the better off you will be. And that inner confidence, which ensures that you don't *accidentally* do a daft deal, usually comes from having your alternative landing site clearly identified. In the case of a negotiation, this isn't just a worst case scenario. It should be kept in mind to judge when your "Goal" is no longer considered achievable.

In fact in all areas of life having thought through planned and committed to paper, what you will do if the current "Plan A" doesn't work out will make you become much more self assured in the way you behave. As a professional seller, the LIYBP in my back pocket has always been having many projects on the boil. This means that when one collapses (as they always do for reasons way beyond my control) I have many other projects to turn to. As a one time *buyer* of services, whilst I was living in New York, ranging through advertising, copywriting, printing, conference organizing, bulk hotel room booking, I always made sure that I had many suppliers in each sector who could really provide me with the service I required.

Also remember that they may also have planned their own LIYBP so try and assess what that might be. But never forget it is only your best assessment. They probably haven't actually told you that this is what they plan to do if things don't work out so you can't totally bank on it. Think through a number of ways in which you could react then prioritise them into the most practical order.

3. IMPALE YOUR PRIORITIES

It is rarely just "the money". Experienced and successful negotiators know that the reason they are sitting here in the first place isn't just to "haggle". There is usually a range of things to be discussed and bargained over and they don't all have the same weighting. And your side's weighting may be very different from the other side's. It is surprising how many managers fail to do this weighting assessment with something as important as employee remuneration for example.

Ask a manager who is about to sit down to negotiate new employee "pay and conditions" and the research shows that over and over again they believe that the weighting (highest to lowest) looks like this, from the employee point of view: 1. Money. 2. Job security. 3. Promotion prospects. 4. Working conditions. 5. Interesting work. 6. Loyalty from the company. 7. Tactful disciplining procedures. 8. Public appreciation for work done. 9. Sympathy for problems. 10. "Inside track" on what's going on.

And yet with a little more research and inner self questioning (placing themselves in the other side's shoes) they might, more correctly, assess that the real employee weighting is usually more like this: 1. Public appreciation for work done. 2. "Inside track" on what's going on. 3. Sympathy for problems 4. Job security. 5. Money. 6. Interesting work. 7. Promotion prospects. 8. Loyalty from the company. 9. Working conditions. 10. Tactful disciplining procedures.

So very careful, prior consideration (especially from the other side's point of view) of all the bargainable elements that could arise, is an important step for all successful negotiators to dwell on. And it is a task that no virgin negotiator can afford to skip over.

The best way for you to begin to impale and weigh the priorities is in a table format.

- *First*, once again using the S.W.O.T table as a foundation, note down all the elements that could come up without considering how important they are or whether you might concede on any of them.
- *Second* (as with the employee motivators above) place yourself in the shoes of the other party and write down any other elements they might want to discuss.
- *Third* give each element a weighting as far as your side is concerned. As with the old 80/20 rule, agreement on the top 20% of items will probably give you 80% of the result you want, so if there are many bargaining chips on the table, after prioritising the top four or five, give all the rest a broad grading *Middle* or *Low*.
- *Fourth* give weightings from their (probable) point of view to each element you have written down. Remember these aren't strange beings from Mars. Their fundamental human drivers are the same as yours. So take care over this process using all the market intelligence and information you have gained so far and your basic experience of being human.

It is so worthwhile doing this because it greatly reduces the chance that your counterparty will raise something unexpected. I once heard, just before a negotiation for a training programme, that a key item for the client would be simply our, "reliability". A track record of just "showing up", "delivering what we said we would" and "not giving any trouble", were all areas in which previous contractors had let them down. So we made sure that we were in a position to "prove" our abilities with references and

Bargainable elements	Our side's priorities	Their side's priorities
Training fee	2	3
Contract length	1	Medium
Tailored modules	4	Medium
Training materials	Medium	4
Licensing agreements	3	2
Performance guarantees	Low	1

financial guarantees at the table which for us was a very easy bargaining point.

Listing all these bargaining points also increases the likelihood that you will achieve that old negotiators dream, "a win-win outcome". This is because of all the things, apart from money, that you have identified as bargaining chips.

Always make sure when you carry out this process of, "impaling your top priorities" that you compare them with your negotiating "Goal" to ensure that both are consistent.

For example if your Goal is: "**We need** to get an obvious win-win in this negotiation **because** this client will still employ us if the predicted industry recession transpires next year", then a priority rating of "1" for your "Training fee", might be inconsistent and require reconsideration before beginning the negotiation.

4. TARGETS

In the "school of hard knocks", I've learnt that being too enthusiastic and eager to please "management" at the "securing a mandate" stage is not good. It has often meant that I have had to return for a new mandate when my prior optimism has proved unachievable. For this reason I always make sure that my targets are now much more flexible in nature.

Rather than saying, *"I am not going to give anything greater than a 7% discount."* I now say, *"If I can get them to concentrate on the 'reliability guarantee', I might then get them to agree 5% but I would actually go to 10% if they agreed to 150 days training in the next three years. But nobody gets more than 10%."*

In doing this I set my negotiating envelope with the highest and lowest limits I believe I can achieve. So when I get to the table I have already negotiated with myself and am working to my own (personal) mandate.

As negotiating, by its very nature, means that I must have this ability to vary the terms during the bargaining process having them predetermined makes life a lot easier. By the way, beware of opening your negotiation by letting the other side know from the outset that "10%" is as far as you will be prepared to go. If you do you will find that is what you will end up giving them. Make them squeeze it out of you!

If you know your market well you should be able to make a reasonable assessment of where your counterparty is likely to

Targets			
Best	Probable	Worst	Theirs
300K	250K	170K	170K
3 Years	2 Years	1 Years	1 Years
10%	7%	5%	10%
Fixed for 3 years no renegotiation	Renegotiable if RPI exceeds 4%	Renegotiable after 12 months	Renegotiable after 12 months

settle. It will also be possible to see where there might be some problems.

In my training business it is always a target for me to have the ability, in long term contracts, to renegotiate terms if inflation takes a turn for the worse over the three or more years. My clients on the other hand would, naturally enough, like everything set in stone so that they know well in advance what their training costs for a project will be. This generally requires some "creativity" on both sides so that we all end up with a "win".

5. CONCESSIONARY COSTS

"Never create a precedent." One of my colleagues in the financial information industry, where I spent the bulk of my employed life, had that motto as a little sign on his desk. Agreeing a deal with one party that is currently unavailable to your other clients is a dangerous move. When the word gets out (oh and it *does* get out!) that they've got a special deal from you without having to trade it for something on their part, you will have a number of angry customers calling you.

> It's not me who can't keep a secret ... It's the people I tell that can't!
>
> *Abraham Lincoln*

So when you are deciding how much a particular concession may cost you, it can be much more than money! Reputation, Forthrightness, Trustworthiness, are all very important considerations in business. So much business is won on recommendation that none of us can risk being caught out. What you offer to one you MUST be prepared to offer to all on the same trading basis: I'll do this for you if you do this for me.

When it comes to concessionary discounts I am always surprised how little sales and negotiating people know about the profitability of the products and services they sell. It may seem easy to give away a 5 %, 7% or even 10%, discount to secure the business, but when you take a look at the full list of fixed and variable costs that have to be factored in before profit is added on top it can be alarming.

For example a product or service with a unit price of $1000 may be compiled of $800 in costs leaving $200 for profit. If the negotiator then agrees to a 10% discount on the whole price they have effectively cut the profit by 50%! And to keep the business ticking along in a normal commercial enterprise, "profit" is all we have to provide our pay, pensions, holidays, dividends and all that unimportant stuff.

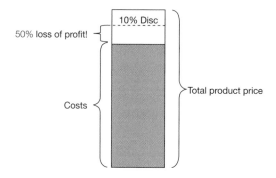

So make quite sure you have calculated the cost of your concessions before you sit down to negotiate. Look at every variable and calculate the cost of conceding and calculate how far you can go. And not just in monetary terms.

6. HEART

Well, here you are at the end of the book.

Negotiation isn't that difficult provided you have prepared adequately, done your homework and have the "Aspiration" to emerge successfully from the other side with what you want.

As you can see, having the confidence to sit down and negotiate takes time; mostly the time you need to invest in "prior preparation". Is this negotiation, the one you are about to embark on, worth the time and effort to you?

Do you have the Heart?

When you get to the table all sorts of ploys may be used against you to get you to invest more time. The other side may try to construct the dreaded "deadline" to make you feel that time is running out. All of this is designed to wear you out more often than not. But all the time they are coming back to the table YOU have something they want ... remember that. As with military campaigns they may try to break your spirit, *"Look you want to go home ... we all want to go home ... so let's agree this now and stop messing about."*

STOP!

Do you have the Heart?

Does where you are now match your Goal? You're a "virgin negotiator" maybe but hey, what's that bulge you can feel in your back pocket? Ah yes you have the LIYBP so you feel confident! So is it walk or stay?

"I mean we're offering you £90K which may be less than you were hoping for but ... we'll see how you get on with this first project and then maybe ..."

If you concede how much will you lose? Look at those calculations again. For £90K you need a five year contract otherwise it doesn't make sense.

"I'll tell you what if we can agree today at £90K we will offer you – in writing a speaking slot at the industry conference in Dubai next month. The main corporate decision makers will be there; 200 of them from around the world ..."

Right your Goal is to expand in this business and they've just offered you a golden chance. The money is just at the bottom end of the target range but the speaker opportunity sits exactly where you set one high end target. If you can now agree the renegotiation terms ... YES.

You have the HEART!!
Keep going ... you are a "virgin" no more.
I look forward to hearing about your success!

P.S. Never enter into a negotiation unless you *aspire* to emerge from it with the very best possible deal you can imagine.

About the Author

Bob Etherington has been developing his reputation for sales success since the 1970s, in a career that has spanned many global markets.

Having begun his career in 1970 with Rank Xerox in London, he was quickly headhunted by Grand Metropolitan Hotels and then became a Money Broker in the City. He joined Reuters, the international news and financial information leader in the 1980s, and became a main Board Director for Transaction Services in 1990, moving to New York in 1994 to take control of their major accounts strategy for US banks. Reuters' international sales to these banks grew rapidly and, as a result, Bob was appointed to organise professional sales training for the entire company.

In 2000, Bob left Reuters and became co-founder of SpokenWord Ltd., the UK-based sales training company. He resigned as Managing Director of SpokenWord Ltd. in 2008.

Bob now lives between his homes in London and Kent and is currently working on a variety of business, theatre and charity projects. He can be contacted at robertetherington@yahoo.co.uk or via the website www.bobetheringtongroup.com.